# Colour
## in Your Garden
## All the Year
## Round

# Colour in Your Garden All the Year Round

## DAVID POPLE

Sundial

# CONTENTS

First published in 1981 by
Octopus Books Limited
59 Grosvenor Street London W1

© 1981 Hennerwood Publications Limited

ISBN 0 906320 76 3

Printed in England by Severn Valley Press Limited

The distribution of plants in this garden is untypical in that the various types – hardy annuals, ornamental shrubs, broad-leaved trees, and so on – are placed in separate groups (see key on page 8); not all the plants shown, moreover, would be in flower at the same time. The drawings that form the title spreads of the chapters represent enlargements of the relevant areas of this master drawing. For example, the drawing that opens the Bedding Plants chapter (pages 32–3) corresponds to the extreme right-hand corner of this picture. The page succeeding each chapter opener contains a key identifying each plant shown in the drawing.

# Introduction

## 8 Introduction

This key plan identifies the plants shown in the drawing on pages 6–7. Hardy annuals: 1 Pot marigold (Calendula), 2 Stock (Malcolmia), 3 Candytuft (Iberis), 4 Scarlet flax (Linum), 5 Cornflower (Centaurea), 6 Clary (Salvia), 7 Poached-egg flower (Limnanthes), 8 California poppy (Eschscholzia).

Bedding plants: 9 planted pots, 10 Fibrous-rooted begonia, 11 White alyssum (Lobularia), 12 Phlox, 13 Tobacco plant (Nicotiana), Chrysanthemum.

Hardy border plants: 15 Cranes' bill (Geranium), 16 Lungwort (Pulmonaria), 17 Plantain lily (Hosta), 18 Phlox, 19 Peony (Paeonia), 20 Pink (Dianthus), 21 Coreopsis, 22 Physalis, 23 Honesty (Lunaria), 24 Michaelmas daisy (Aster), 25 Stonecrop (Sedum), 26 Lamb's tongue (Stachys), 27 Columbine (Aquilegia), 28 Japanese anemone (Anemone x hybrida), 29 Russell lupins (Lupinus), 30 Yarrow (Achillea), 31 Catmint (Nepeta), 32 Larkspur (Delphinium).

Evergreens: 33 Lawson's cypress (Chamaecyparis), 34 Sawara cypress (Chamaecyparis), 35 Juniper (Juniperus 'Pfitzeriana Aurea'), 36 C. lawsoniana 'Pottenii', 37 C. l. 'Green Pillar', 38 C. l. 'Culumnaris', 39 Westfelton yew (Taxus), 40 Colorado spruce (Picea), 41 C. l. 'Kilmacurragh', 42 Winter heathers (Erica), 43 Daphne, 44 Holly (Ilex).

Broad-leaved trees: 45 Hawthorn (Crataegus), 46 Crab-apple bush (Malus), 47 Coral-bark maple (Acer), 48 Japanese maple (Acer), 49 Snowy mespilus (Amelanchier), 50 Weeping cotoneaster, 51 Willow-leaved pear (Pyrus), 52 Ornamental shrubs, 52 Viburnum, 53 Shrub rose, 54 Oregon grape (Mahonia), 55 Jerusalem sage (Phlomis), 56 Dogwood (Cornus), 57 Flowering quince (Chaenomeles), 58 Buddleia, 59 Forsythia, 60 Lavender (Lavandula).

Ground-cover plants: 61 Rock cress (Aubrieta), 62 Yellow alyssum, 63 Plantain lily (Hosta), 64 Rue (Ruta), 65 Periwinkle (Vinca), 66 Thrift (Armeria), 67 Candytuft (Iberis), 68 Waldsteinia, 69 Festuca, 70 Marjoram (Origanum), 71 Bugle (Ajuga), 72 Bergenia, 73 Christmas rose (Helleborus).

Climbing and wall shrubs: 74 Tassel bush (Garrya), 75 Winter-flowering jasmine (Jasminum), 76 Clematis, 77 Honeysuckle (Lonicera), 78 Japanese crimson glory vine (Vitis coignetiae), 79 Chinese wisteria.

Hedges: 80 Holly (Ilex), 81 Barberry (Berberis darwinii), 82 Rose ('Queen Elizabeth', floribunda), 83 Beech (Fagus).

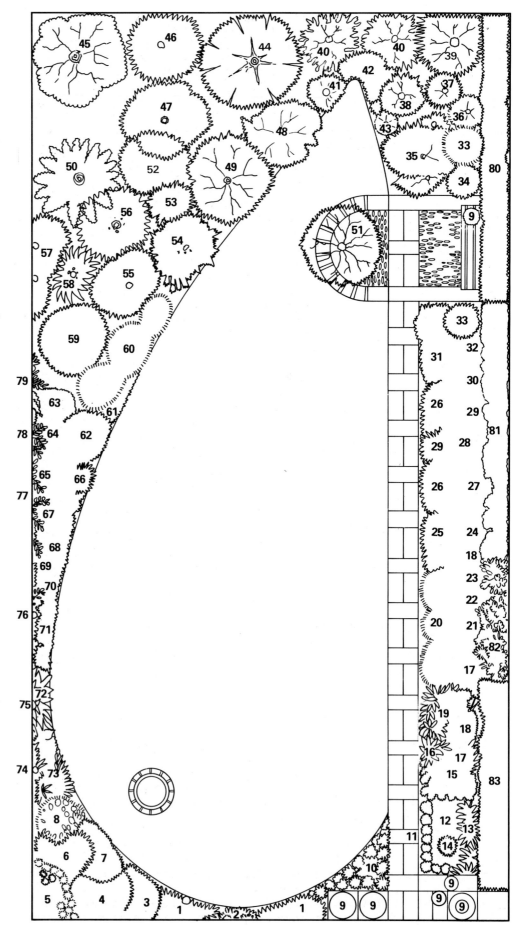

The discovery that it is posssible to have a bright and lively garden the year round comes as a delightful surprise to many people. For although bare dripping branches and a dark, windblown conifer may be pleasing to some, most people would prefer to have their spirits raised by a winter view of differing shapes, colours, and tints. Spring, summer, and autumn will readily produce succeeding pageants of colour, but with careful planting the garden will offer pleasing shapes and colours in winter as well. There is no need to have an off-season: even January can have a charm of its own if you plant with a winter wonderland in mind. Flowers will be few and delicate at that time, but if the setting is attractive you will be tempted outdoors to inspect them closely.

Although the most brilliant colours are generally provided by flowers, coloured foliage makes an important contribution to the scene. And because leaves, especially those of evergreen shrubs and trees, are with us far longer than any flowers, they should form a vital feature of your overall colour plans. (The term 'evergreen' is applied to any plant that has a full quota of foliage in winter and summer alike. We tend to think of evergreens in terms of a dark-green colour. In fact, they exhibit great variety: some are bright green; others have grey, blue, or yellow foliage – sometimes quite brilliant – which shines out in the dull winter days.)

The smaller the area of your garden, the greater is the need to look out for plants that offer more than one claim to attention. An obvious example is those that follow their flowering period with a colourful crop of fruits or berries. Others noted for their flowers may have specially attractive foliage that lasts all summer long. Where possible, different types of plants should be grown in association so that you get two or three lots of colour from the same area. Such happy groupings are discovered by observation and experiment – which is why visiting other gardens, private and public, can be so rewarding.

It is essential to get the mix right when selecting your plants. One way to ensure a garden of colour the year round would be to fill it with colourful conifers, but it would be terribly monotonous because it would offer very little variation between one season and another. In general it is better to restrict evergreens to about one in four of the trees and shrubs planted. The same principle applies to plants with bright-coloured, and especially variegated, leaves: attractive though these are, it's always possible to have too much of a good thing.

Positioning is also most important, not only to ensure that the areas of colour are spread throughout the garden, and those that might clash are kept well apart, but also to place some winter flowerings, for instance, where they can be viewed from your windows.

In the following chapters I describe some of the delightful plants that can help you create a garden that will be colourful throughout the year. None of those mentioned should be difficult to grow or hard to come by, although you may not find all of them at your local garden centre or nursery. Most are happy in ordinary garden soil; a few, however, flourish only in acid soil, and this is clearly indicated in each case.

Any perennial plant you buy is an investment, something that can pay dividends in the form of beauty and interest for many years, provided that the soil is well prepared, that you sow (or plant) it properly, and then give it such little aftercare as it may need. Remember that a plant's roots may be as extensive as its top growth. While we can do all sorts of things for the part above ground, there is very little we can do for the roots once they are buried in the soil; hence the need for special care when planting. And if this seems to be rather time-consuming, remember that it has to be done only once for permanent plants. Even a whole hour spent giving a tree a good start in life is very little when you consider how many years of enjoyment you can expect from it.

Many people do not realise that roots need air to breathe in order to thrive. This is usually present in adequate amounts by the natural state of things, provided the soil does not become waterlogged. Where drainage is bad, water blocks the air spaces in the soil with the result that roots are killed by suffocation. On the other hand, as well as being well drained, the soil must be capable of holding sufficient moisture to sustain plants through long dry periods.

## Soil

The major part of soil is made up of a mixture of mineral particles of varying sizes, ranging from stones and gravel, down through coarse and fine sand to silts, and finally to the smallest of all, the microscopic particles of clay. The soil behaves in different ways depending on which size of particle predominates. Gravelly and sandy soils tend to be light, free-draining, and therefore dry in summer, and they provide little in the way of plant food. At the other extreme, heavy clay soils are poor-draining, sticky, and difficult to work when wet, hold a great deal of moisture, and are potentially rich in plant foods. A good mixture of particle sizes results in what gardeners call a loam. This is neither so free-draining and dry as sandy soils, nor as heavy, wet, and poorly aerated as clay ones.

The mineral part of the soil holds water in the form of a surface layer of moisture around each particle, any surplus draining away through the gaps between them. The bigger the gaps are, the better the drainage and the easier it is for air to penetrate. If you imagine a jar of marbles compared with a jar of granulated sugar you will realise what a difference particle size makes to the gaps between them.

These gaps can be increased on heavy clay soils, so improving their drainage, if individual particles can be made to group together to form crumbs. The development of a crumb structure can be brought about by humus. This is a dark substance derived from the breakdown of organic matter, mainly plant and animal debris, and it forms the second major constituent of soil.

The natural supply of humus is reduced to very little on clean, cultivated land, especially in a tidy garden. Moreover, cultivation increases the supply of air to the soil and thus hastens the final disintegration of what humus there is. Gardeners therefore need to make good the supply by adding bulky organic material, such as farmyard manure, hop or mushroom manure, garden compost, or similar material.

Conversion of this organic material to humus is carried out by the unseen third constituent of fertile soil, its teeming population of micro-organisms. As a result of this process of decomposition, the organic material releases substances that plants use for food. The speed of the breaking-down process depends partly on the soil temperature and the amount of oxygen available. In poorly aerated, cooler clays it may take several years for a dressing of manure to disappear completely; in a hot, sandy soil it may vanish within a year.

Humus not only makes soil fertile; it also improves its structure. In free-draining sandy soils it holds moisture and foodstuffs at depths that are within reach of plant roots, while in heavy clays it improves drainage and makes them warmer and easier to work. There are various other methods of improving the structure of heavy soils. Horticultural gypsum improves clay soils by causing the particles to flocculate (group together). Hydrated lime sweetens the soil my making it less acid, and it also provides calcium, an important plant food. (Lime must not be used indiscriminately, however, because an excess may interfere with the ability of plants to absorb certain essential substances, especially iron.)

*The touch of rich red provided by a few bedding geraniums (Pelargonium) in a large pot makes a delightful contrast with the pale yellow flowers of lady's mantle (Alchemilla mollis) and brings life to this small corner in summer.*

One of the greatest improvers of heavy clay soils is a natural one – frost. The microscopic clay particles are plate-like in shape and stick together after the manner of wet sheets of glass. By freezing and expanding the water, however, frost causes the particles to be pushed apart and upsets their alignment. A clay soil which is turned over in large clods in autumn and exposed to hard winter frosts can be broken down easily the following spring to create a tilth – a layer of fine soil – suitable for seed sowing. Walking on and so compressing such a soil when it is wet, however, quickly destroys this texture and can reduce it to the consistency of plasticine.

In general, plants that grow well on an alkaline (limy or chalky) soil will also flourish when planted in one that is slightly acid. But others, such as rhododendrons (including azaleas) and most heaths and heathers, that demand acid soil will not tolerate even a mildly alkaline one. Any hint of chalk or lime around their roots will upset them, and their leaves will turn yellow. The first step before choosing plants for a new garden must therefore be to determine whether the soil is acid or alkaline.

You can do this with one of the inexpensive soil-testing kits available at most garden centres. While excessive acidity is easily corrected by mixing lime with the soil (preferably in the autumn prior to spring plantings), it is extremely difficult to make an alkaline soil acid. Undoubtedly a moderately acid soil makes life much easier for anyone wanting to grow the widest variety of plants and is, of course, essential if your want to grow acid-loving ones.

**Preparation for Planting**

Armed with the result of the soil test, you can set about preparing the ground of your plot for planting. If it is a new garden, the first job is to clear away any surface rubbish and dig the whole area, turning over the ground to the full depth of a spade's blade. At the same time organic material can be buried in the trenches, together with any weeds or grass skimmed from the soil surface as the work proceeds. Remove any old tree roots or rubble you may find. If you do this work in autumn or winter, leave the surface rough and open to weather until spring, when it can be broken down and levelled. If the work must be done in spring or summer and the plot is needed for immediate planting, the soil must be broken up finely with the aid of a fork when digging. (Alternatively you can hire a machine cultivator or use the services of a garden contractor.)

Refurbishing an existing garden is often bedevilled by the presence of perennial

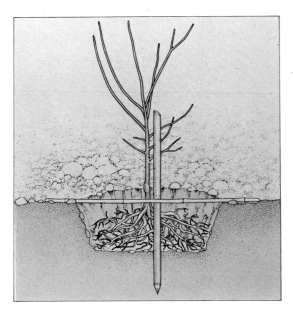

*When planting a tree ensure the hole is deep enough for the old soil mark on the stem to finish at soil level. Use a cane laid across the hole to line up the soil mark.*

*Work peat in among the roots before returning the soil so as to provide a reservoir of moisture and to encourage the development of new roots.*

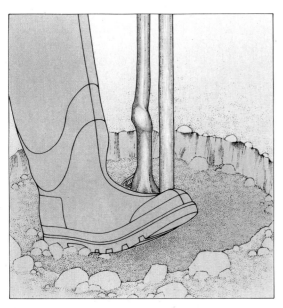

*Really firm planting is essential to success. Return the soil in layers and compress each one with with your heel, putting your full weight on it.*

weeds. It is no use burying them or cutting them down as they will quickly reappear. If weeds such as couch grass, bindweed, and ground elder abound they should be killed with a herbicide before digging the soil. If it is necessary to dispose of any ailing shrubs or old trees to make room for new ones, remove as much of their roots as you can.

To ensure the new plants get away to a flying start, the soil should be enriched with plant foods 10 to 14 days before sowing or planting. The easiest method is to spread a general fertiliser over the area at the maximum rate recommended and mix it into the surface of the soil with a fork or tined cultivator. Follow this by treading over the whole area, shuffling up and down and across it, keeping your feet close together and your weight on your heels. Failure to refirm ground in this way results in it being too well aerated, so that it will tend to dry out quickly.

The final stage of preparation is to level the surface by raking. Where plants are to go it is sufficient just to erase your footprints, but where you intend to sow seeds you must do a more thorough raking job. In order to grow satisfactorily, seeds must be in intimate contact with the soil so that they can absorb the moisture needed to trigger germination. What is required is a layer, about 25 mm (1 in) deep, of finely broken down soil from which all large stones and plant debris have been combed out. If the ground is lumpy you may need to tread and rake it several times to produce the required fine tilth.

**Planting Procedures**
Having the largest roots, trees and shrubs involve the most work in planting. Deciduous ones that have been lifted from the soil and sent out with bare roots from nurseries should be planted during their dormant period, which lasts from the time the leaves fall in autumn until about mid-March. Within this period, however, it is preferable to plant in autumn, before the ground becomes really cold. This will enable the plants to make some new root growth then, although they will of course remain leafless until the spring.

Before planting any tree or shrub, make sure that its roots are moist. If they appear to be dry, soak them in a bucket of water. Now check them for any damage and remove any broken or skinned root ends, cutting back to sound tissue. Extra-long roots can be shortened to match the others in length.

The technique of planting dormant trees and shrubs is shown in the drawings at left. Other perennial plants moved in winter should be planted in the same way, although it is better to firm in smaller plants with your knuckles or the trowel handle.

Pressing soil firmly into contact with roots is the essence of good planting. Plants will not root well into loose soil, which also (as we have seen) tends to dry out quickly.

Plants that have been grown in pots can be bought and planted out at any time. When the pot is removed, you will find that the roots are enclosed in a ball of soil. The top of this ball must finish level with or just below the surface of the ground soil, and the hole should be big enough to allow you to pack moist peat around the ball before filling in with soil. Again, make sure the soil is quite firm.

Bare-rooted plants usually manage to gather enough water from the soil to supply their moisture needs, except under very dry conditions. A pot-grown one, however, especially if it is in leaf, cannot do so – its entire root system is within the ball, which holds insufficient water to supply its needs for long. It is important, therefore, to water planted-out pot-grown plants until they have had time for their roots to grow and penetrate the soil around them. It is specially important to ensure the roots and soil are moist before planting out, so water the pots an hour or two beforehand. If it is exceptionally dry I find it best to stand the pots in a bucket of water for a little while to soak thoroughly.

Drying out of the surrounding soil just as the new roots are developing can cause a severe check to any young plant. For trees and shrubs, especially, it is wise to spread a layer of peat or compost over the ground around them as a mulch. This will reduce surface evaporation and so conserve moisture. A mulch 50 mm (2 in) deep or so will also smother germinating weed seedlings, an important consideration since weeds take both moisture and foods that developing plants need as well as physically smother small plants. The need to prevent competition is the reason why a circle of bare soil at least 600 mm (2 ft) across should be maintained around new shrubs and trees for the first few years, even when they are planted in a lawn.

Once they are established, healthy long-lived plants require regular but simple maintenance. Some trees and shrubs may need a little pruning to keep them shapely; others, such as hybrid tea roses, will need more rigorous pruning. You must, of course, inspect your plants frequently for signs of pests or diseases. Weeding, too, must be carried out regularly, although it will become less of a chore after a few seasons.

*After flowering, many of the deciduous shrubs make a second important contribution to garden colour as their leaves take on fiery tints in the shortening autumn days.*

Calendar

# Spring

## MARCH

Bulbs make an important impact on the garden scene this month, as the winter-flowering crocuses flower in profusion and the blue, mauve, and purple cultivars of *Iris reticulata* come into full bloom, together with chionodoxas, *Scilla sibirica*, *Anemone blanda*, and the first daffodils (*Narcissus*). Later-flowering cultivars of the winter-flowering heathers (*Erica*) break into bloom this month, taking over from those that started in December and January. Forsythias open their yellow bells and the yellow Oregon grape (*Mahonia aquifolium*) and bright red and pink flowering quinces (*Chaenomeles*) begin blooming. Lungworts (*Pulmonaria*) produce flowers of red, pink, and blue to start off a new season, while the earliest leopard's bane (*Doronicum*) opens the first yellow daisies.

Finish putting in border plants and lifted trees and shrubs as soon as possible. Shear off the dead flower-heads from those winter-flowering heathers that have finished blooming, in order to keep them compact. Take cuttings of delphiniums and lupins as soon as the shoots are about 100 mm (4 in) high. Make sure each has a solid base, and set them in pots of rooting compost in a frame. Scatter general fertiliser around hardy border plants and roses and mix it into the soil surface. Towards the end of the month prune climbing roses and hypericums; also deal with hybrid tea and floribunda roses and *Buddleia davidii* before the month is out. Layer shoots of deciduous shrubs to make new plants, before their leaves get in your way. Plant a batch of gladioli for early flowers.

## APRIL

Daffodils and narcissi make a brave show this month, together with the early tulips, blue grape hyacinths, and the majestic crown imperials (*Fritillaria*). Yellow leopard's bane flowers make a sunny display and are joined by *Omphalodes cappadocica*, epimediums, bergenias, and the earliest-flowering ajugas. Perennial yellow alyssum, purple to red aubrieta, and white arabis make masses of colour wherever grown as ground cover. The periwinkles (*Vinca*) start flowering in earnest this month, as do evergreen barberries (*Berberis*) and Jew's mallow (*Kerria japonica*), while the flowering crab-apples (*Malus*) and snowy mespilus (*Amelanchier*) cover themselves in blossom and the early-flowering brooms (*Cytisus*) burst into colour.

Sow seeds of hardy annuals to flower in summer. Also, sow seeds of perennial border plants, such as oriental poppies (*Papaver*), lupins, and coral flower (*Heuchera*) in a prepared seedbed out of doors if a lot of plants are needed cheaply. They are rarely up to the quality of named varieties, but help stock a new garden until better plants can be afforded. Plant gladioli for the main summer display. Start staking quick-growing border plants, such as delphiniums. Late April is a

*Key to plants, pages 14–5: 1 Christmas rose (*Helleborus niger*), 2 Winter aconite (*Eranthis hyemalis*), 3 Winter-flowering jasmine (*Jasminum nudiflorum*), 4 Snowdrop (*Galanthus nivalis*), 5 Bergenia crassifolia.*

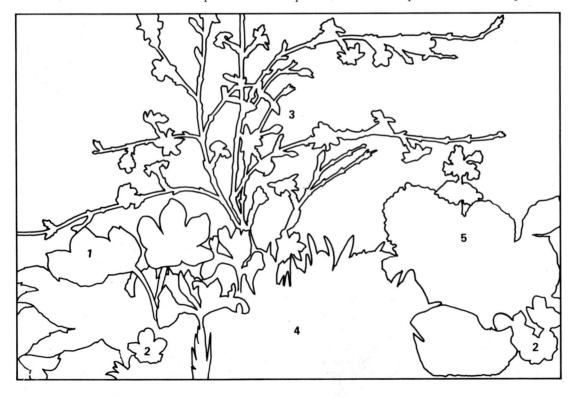

good time to put in evergreen trees and shrubs, including conifers. Make sure they do not dry out after planting, and syringe them with water in the evenings of dry days. Prune forsythias and other spring-flowering shrubs, if necessary, when their display has finished. From now until autumn trees, shrubs, and plants that have been raised in containers can be successfully established, but they will need to be watered whenever the soil around their roots begins to dry out. Keep down weeds by hoeing or treating the soil with a paraquat weedkiller.

## MAY

Late narcissi are joined by regiments of colourful tulips and the bluebell *Endymion hispanicus* (syn. *Scilla campanulata*). The pretty cultivars of the dead-nettle (*Lamium maculatum*) produce their pink spikes, which go well with the variegated leaves. By now all the plants grown for their foliage – silver artemisias and lamb's tongue (*Stachys lanata*), the hostas in wide array, the brilliant ajugas, the variegated and yellow- and purple-leaved

shrubs – are contributing colour to the scene. Masses of blossom are provided by Japanese cherries (*Prunus*), the flowering thorns (*Crataegus*), wisterias, and *Clematis montana*.

Thin out and weed hardy annuals sown earlier and support the taller ones; continue staking and tying border plants as they grow. Prune the early, small-flowered clematis, flowering quinces (*Chaenomeles*), and other shrubs when they have finished blooming. Watch out for attacks of greenfly and other pests from now on and spray with insecticide to control them as soon as they appear. About the middle of May dormant dahlia tubers can be planted in the garden. If you want to divide them use a knife and split the clumps so that each tuber has a small section of the old stem attached; it is from the area close to the stem that the new shoots arise. Towards the end of the month half-hardy bedding plants can be set out in mild areas where danger of further frost is unlikely. Check regularly to make sure newly planted evergreens and container-grown plants are not suffering from drought.

*Tulips (Tulipa) and wallflowers (Cheiranthus), two of the most reliable spring flowers, are easily combined to provide a scintillating show in May.*

# Summer

## JUNE

A whole host of hardy border plants, such as pinks (*Dianthus*), delphiniums, lupins, peonies, day lilies, and oriental poppies, burst into flower this month, together with many of the hardy annuals sown earlier. New shrubs to flower include the early Dutch honeysuckle (*Lonicera*), potentillas, weigelas, hypericums, the climbing hydrangea, the potato-tree (*Solanum crispum*), jasmine night-shade (*Solanum jasminoides*), *Buddleia alternifolia*, and *B. globosa*. One of the glories of June, however, is the roses, which make a tremendous show of colour – even those planted the previous autumn and spring making a fine display.

Complete planting beds and borders with tender plants, including dahlias, cannas, and other bedding plants, as early as possible. Trim back brooms (*Cytisus*), aubrieta, and heathers (*Erica*) as they finish flowering to keep them bushy. Check upright conifers to ensure that they have not produced competing shoots at the top. Remove dead flowers from roses, annuals, and border plants as they fade. Keep a look out for suckers growing from the roots of budded or grafted plants, including roses and witch hazels (*Hamamelis*), and remove any as soon as you notice them. Conserve moisture by mulching the soil around plants when it is wet, covering it with a 50 mm (2 in) layer of garden compost, rotted manure, peat, or other suitable material. Divide and transplant any bearded irises that have become overcrowded as soon as they finish flowering. Loosely tie in to their supports the new, whippy shoots of rambler roses to prevent them being blown about and damaged.

## JULY

The butterfly bush (*Buddleia davidii*) blooms in July, together with hypericums, the daisy bush (*Olearia* × *hastii*), Jerusalem sage (*Phlomis fruticosa*), the climbing *Schizofragma integrifolia*, many of the later-flowering, large clematis cultivars, and the dainty yellow *Clematis tangutica*. Extra colour is provided in borders by white *Chrysanthemum maximum*, the pink, daisy-like cone flower (*Echinacea*), the blazing star (*Liatris*), and knotweeds (*Polygonum*). Border phloxes also burst upon the summer scene together with the brilliant purple *Salvia nemorosa*, dwarf dahlias, and all the summer bedding plants.

Continue dead-heading border plants and annuals to keep them tidy and flowering.

*Roses and other hardy plants can be grown together to produce an abundance of summer flowers even in a narrow border such as this.*

Keep tying in large dahlias (their brittle stems are easily damaged) as well as the later-flowering border plants. Hardy geraniums that have flopped over after flowering can be cut to the ground and will produce fresh foliage. Prune wisterias and weigelas when they, too, finish flowering. Order bulbs for autumn planting. Feed roses with fertiliser when the first flush of blooms had faded; this will improve the later display. Layer stems of clematis into pots of soil to increase your stock: two-year-old or older wood roots best. Keep bedding and other plants well watered in dry spells, giving the soil a thorough soaking each time with the aid of a hose pipe and sprinkler. Any heavy cutting of evergreen hedges is best done now so that the resultant new growth has time to harden before winter arrives.

## AUGUST

The dainty Japanese anemones, golden rod (*Solidago*) ice plants, and tuberous dahlias take over the display in beds and borders as earlier plants pass out of bloom. The knotweeds (*Polygonum*) show their advantages now and the charming dwarf *Cyclamen neapolitanum* adds to the display. It is also the month when the spectacular *Campsis* × *tagliabuana* opens its red trumpet flowers after a hot summer, and the bedding plants reach the peak of their display, as do some late cultivars and species of clematis.

Plant early-flowering bulbs, such as crocuses, fritillarias, chionodoxas, the dwarf bulbous irises, daffodils, and narcissi for a display next spring. Also set out autumn crocus (*Colchicum*) bulbs as soon as they arrive. Continue to dead-head roses, buddleias, and border plants. Cutting off the spikes of *Salvia nemorosa* just above the top leaves on each stem will encourage a good second display. Shrubs and hardy plants ordered for autumn planting should begin to arrive this month. Cuttings of many hardy shrubs can be rooted in a frame, or outdoors under a bottomless box covered over at the top with clear polythene. Use side-shoots 100–150 mm (4–6 in) long, pulled off with a heel of older wood at the base. Keep them moist until rooted. Clear away hardy annuals that have finished flowering before they shed too many seeds. Lightly trim lavenders (*Lavandula*) with shears to keep them compact, but do not cut into the old wood. Give a final, light trim to any evergreen hedges that need it.

# Autumn

### SEPTEMBER

Many berrying trees and shrubs add extra colour at this time, including cotoneasters, pernettyas, cultivars of the mountain ash (*Sorbus*), and the firethorns (*Pyracantha*). Some of the first glowing autumn leaf colouring is provided by the snowy mespilus (*Amelanchier*). Michaelmas daisies (*Aster*) bring fresh colour to borders and many species and cultivars of the dainty autumn crocuses and colchicums begin flowering, the latter being without leaves, which appear in the spring.

If peonies have to be moved or divided, this is the best time to do it; also the winter-flowering *Iris unguicularis*. From now until mid-October is the second period when lifted conifers and other evergreens can be moved safely. After planting, water them freely in dry weather. Prune rambler roses, removing or shortening the old stems and tying in the new ones to replace them. Many roses, especially ramblers, can be raised from cuttings taken now. Use ripe shoots 150–200 mm (6–8 in) long, inserted to half their depth in a patch of well-drained soil. Shorter shoots of the cotton lavender (*Santolina*) also root well with this treatment. Remove any foliage that would be buried. The tougher hardy annuals, such as calendulas, cornflowers (*Centaurea*), and godetia, can be sown now to provide larger plants and earlier flowers next season. Lift and pot any pelargoniums, tender fuchsias, and cannas you want to save before the first frost arrives; keep them in a warm greenhouse, or in a light place indoors, for the winter.

### OCTOBER

All the trees and shrubs noted for their fiery autumn leaf colour, including the snowy mespilus (*Amelanchier*), *Berberis thunbergii*, Japanese maples (*Acer*), Virginia creepers (*Parthenocissus*), and ornamental vines (*Vitis*), can set the garden ablaze with colour. The diaplay of brilliant berries continues and the brightly coloured crab-apples (*Malus*) add to the show, some hanging on long after the leaves have fallen. Some autumn crocus and colchicum species continue to open their frail blooms and many border plants, such as ice plants and Michaelmas daisies (*Aster*), hold their display well into the month, while others make a second, smaller, but nonetheless welcome showing. The first glistening pink blooms of *Nerine bowdenii* open now, as do the kaffir lilies (*Schizostylis*), and most bedding plants continue to be colourful until cut down by the first autumn frost.

Complete the work of planting all bulbs (except tulips) as soon as possible. Weed any hardy annuals sown last month and thin them out to 75 mm (3 in) apart from the winter. Clear fallen leaves from low-growing plants. Lift and store away gladiolus corms and dahlia tubers once their top growth has been frosted, or at the end of this month. Prepare ground for new plants and set them in place as soon as possible after they arrive. Most border and ground-cover plants can be lifted and divided now and the soil refurbished before they are replanted. In any case borders should be tidied up, old leaves and stems removed, and canes and other supports cleaned and stored away.

## NOVEMBER

As deciduous trees and shrubs shed their remaining leaves, the winter garden scene emerges, but provided it is well planted with evergreens it never looks empty and dead. The coloured-leaved conifers, especially, can provide plenty of variety. Also revealed when the leaves fall is the colourful bark of some trees and shrubs, like that of the coral-bark maple (*Acer*), and this is attractive the whole winter through. Kaffir lilies (*Schizostylis*) and nerines continue to flower, together with a few late autumn crocuses (*Colchicum*). Evergreen ground-cover plants also keep the garden alive, especially those with brightly coloured leaves, such as some of the ajugas and ivies (*Hedera*).

Last of the bulbs to go in are the tulips, which round off the bulb-planting season. Divide and replant overcrowded clumps of lily-of-the-valley (*Convallaria*). Clear away the remains of summer bedding plants and the late-flowering border plants. Gather up fallen leaves and stack them in a wire-netting enclosure to rot down and provide a useful mulching material. Alternatively, add them to a compost heap where all except very woody plant debris can be rotted down to produce a valuable organic fertiliser. Some evergreens, including privet (*Ligustrum*) and laurel (*Prunus*), can be rooted from hardwood cuttings inserted in light soil in a sheltered spot outdoors. Such deciduous shrubs as *Buddleia davidii*, flowering currants, flowering quinces (*Chaenomeles*), and vines can be increased in the same way.

*The effect of autumn colour is greatly enhanced if shrubs are positioned where the low autumn sunlight can shine through their leaves.*

# Winter

## DECEMBER

Chief source of massed colour this month is provided by the foliage of evergreens, particularly those variegated or coloured with gold or yellow, or of a fresh green colour. *Viburnum bodnantense* provides clusters of pink flowers at its shoot tips and the winter-flowering jasmine makes a prominent display with its bright-yellow flowers. Earliest of the winter-flowering heathers (*Erica*), which will have been showing promise for weeks, cover themselves with bright flowers, and the first frail blooms of *Iris unguicularis* can be found nestling amidst their grassy foliage.

Take the opportunity of mild spells to prune leafless shrubs in need of attention. Also plant late-arriving shrubs and plants if the ground is not too wet and sticky: if it is, heel the plants in together in a well-drained spot until conditions improve. Tidy established borders, lightly forking over the soil among the plants. At the same time mix in old mulching material, and add a dressing of manure if available. Feed with bone meal established hedges and areas planted with bulbs. Border plants, such as Japanese anemones, perennial anchusas, and border phloxes, can be propagated from root cuttings taken now. Order seeds for sowing next season; also shrubs and plants to set out in the spring to fill gaps or create new groupings. Cover the soil over plants of doubtful hardiness with straw, bracken, or tree leaves held in place with wire netting, to give extra frost protection in the coming months.

## JANUARY

This is often thought of as a completely colourless month in the garden, but there is quite a number of plants that bloom then. The winter-flowering jasmine (*Jasminum nudiflorum*) is generously spangled with its bright yellow blooms that are continuously produced whenever the weather is mild, and some cultivars of the winter-flowering heather (*Erica*) are smothered in their tiny blooms, shining even through the snow. In milder areas *Garrya elliptica* is hung with its long, silver catkins to give a charming display, snowdrops (*Galanthus*) have appeared in many gardens, and *Iris unguicularis* opens its lilac blooms throughout the winter months. Towards the end of January, winter aconites (*Eranthis hyemalis*) begin to flower in the sunshine to provide a touch of sparkling yellow in sheltered spots. More colour is provided by the bark of some trees and shrubs, none more eyecatching than the brilliant crimson young shoots of the dogwood (*Cornus alba* 'Sibirica'), while the coloured-leaved evergreens, such as the variegated hollies and ivy and the golden conifers, create an impression of sunniness even on overcast days.

Jobs to be done this month include the digging of ground ready for spring sowing and planting, as well as ordering the seeds, shrubs, and plants if this has not already been done. Prune ornamental vines trained on walls and pergolas; also other deciduous trees and shrubs in need of such treatment. If there is a heavy fall of snow, knock it off the branches of conifers and other evergreens; if their shoots are weighed down for long their shape may be spoiled. Make sure that the tender tubers and corms of plants such as dahlias and gladioli are well protected from frost with a mulch.

## FEBRUARY

Although this is often the harshest winter month, cold fails to deter the witch hazels or *Daphne mezereum* from opening their scented flowers now. The winter-flowering heathers continue to bloom profusely, regardless of frost and snow, while the winter-flowering jasmine and *Viburnum × bodnantense* open a fresh crop of flowers as soon as each cold spell passes. The first dainty blooms of the dwarf *Cyclamen orbiculatum* often appear this month and the yellow winter aconites get into their stride if it is sunny. The scented strings of pale yellow *Mahonia japonica* flowers open at the shoot tips, and the first winter crocuses open wide in any warming ray of sun. The dwarf yellow *Iris danfordiae* and blue *I. histrioides* flower, to be joined towards the end of the month by the first few purple blooms of *I. reticulata* in many places.

Retread the soil around newly planted trees and shrubs to firm it again when it dries out after heavy frost. Also push back into the ground any hardwood cuttings of shrubs that have been lifted by frost, and refirm the soil about them. Check posts, pales, trellis, and wires used as plant supports and replace or tighten any that are broken or loose before the plants break into new growth. The end of the month is the time to prune those cultivars of *Cornus alba* grown for the bright winter colouring of their young shoots, to encourage a new crop the following summer. This is the time, too, to prune all clematis plants except the small-flowered ones, such as *Clematis montana*, that bloom early. Shear off the old foliage from the rose of sharon (*Hypericum calycinum*), ivies, and other fast-spreading plants before new growth begins.

*Brilliant red shoots of the Westonbirt dogwood (Cornus alba 'Sibirica'), here set against a background of the yellow-barked dogwood (C. stolonifera 'Flaviramea') for contrast, make a vivid display throughout the winter.*

# Hardy Annuals

Growing hardy annuals as a feature in themselves has gone out of fashion, owing to the small size of most modern gardens and the fact that people prefer a more permanent scheme that does not have to be renewed each season. But for anyone faced with a bare plot and wishing to have colourful flowers quickly, hardy annuals still have much to commend them. Indeed, there is nothing to beat them for providing the maximum amount of colour at minimum cost in the shortest time. They are ideal, too, for growing between shrubs and trees for a season or two until the permanent plants need all the space allotted to them, or for filling any awkward gap that may appear in a bed or border.

To get the best effect, choose those hardy annuals that can provide massed colour. This means excluding plants such as larkspur (*Delphinium*), which, although it is stately and makes an excellent cut flower, does not keep up a long show. You should also take care to position them so that short plants are not hidden behind tall ones and in such a way that those with flowers of similar shades are separated by those of other colours.

If you intend to devote a whole bed or border to hardy annuals alone it is best to sow them in large irregular patches of each kind, rather than a few here and there. Also, arrange them so that the edges of the groups are staggered rather like those of bricks in a wall so that there are no distinct dividing lines running from front to back, or from end to end, of the bed.

It saves time and prevents mistakes if you draw up a rough plan beforehand showing where each variety of annual is to be sown, giving its height and colour. Then, once the ground has been raked and prepared for sowing, the outlines of the different areas can be marked out on the soil and each sown with its allotted plant.

In general hardy annuals are not fussy about the type of soil, making as good a show on sandy ground as they do in clay. It has often been asserted that they flower best on poor soil, although in my experience this is only half true. You get a much more rewarding display from plants that have sufficient food to grow to a proper size. On the other hand, hardy annuals must never be given a lot of fresh manure or nitrogenous fertiliser, such as nitrate of soda, both of which tend to lead to rank growth with luxuriant foliage and poor flowering. I find that if a little general fertiliser, such as the Growmore devised for vegetables, is worked into the ground while preparing it for sowing, this will suit these flowers very well unless the soil is naturally rich. In most cases, however, the key to good flowering is adequate sun.

Hardy annuals vary in size from those that make ground-hugging mats to plants 1 m (3 ft) or more in height, and come in the widest range of colours. If your aim is to be as labour-saving as possible, and especially if your garden is exposed to wind, restrict your choice to those that do not exceed a height of about 400 mm (16 in) to avoid having to support them with canes.

*Key to plants, pages 24–5: 1 Virginian stock (Malcolmia maritima), 2 Pot marigold (Calendula officinalis), 3 Candytuft (Iberis), 4 Scarlet flax (Linum grandiflorum 'Rubrum'), 5 Cornflower (Centaurea cyanus), 6 Poached-egg flower (Limnanthes douglasii), 7 Mixed clary (Salvia horminum), 8 Californian poppies (Eschscholzia californica).*

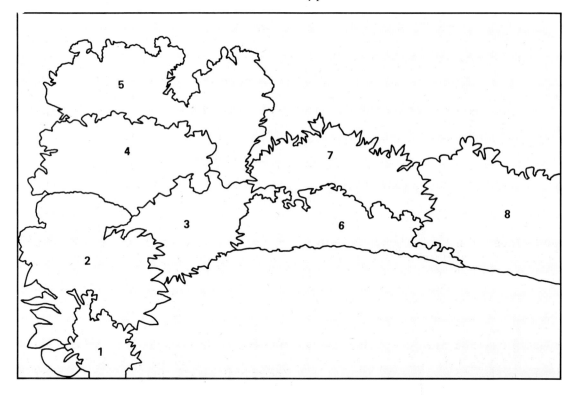

Many of these plants are offered in several distinct colours as well as in mixtures. Where a number of them are being grown in association, my preference is to choose individual colours as far as possible, since too many mixed selections give a spotty effect rather than a rich, bold display. But if a single species of annual is sown in isolation, between some shrubs perhaps, a mixture can be charming.

In recent years some of the old and best-known annual flowers have had their botanical names changed. For instance, the familiar white alyssum, which was as much favoured for edging beds in summer in our grandparents' time as it is today, should now properly be called *Lobularia maritima*, although its old name (*Alyssum maritimum*) is still occasionally to be found. Its common name, 'white alyssum', continues to be used in the seed trade. Where possible, I shall use the names you will find on the seed packets or in nurserymen's catalogues, even though they may have derived from Latin names that have been changed.

**Selection**

Although often raised under glass and sold as a bedding plant, white alyssum is a hardy annual that can be sown in the place where it is to bloom. Each plant makes a tidy mat covered with clusters of small flowers for most of the summer. The seedlings are rather slow to develop at first, but an April sowing of the white cultivars will make a good show from mid-summer onwards. Less vigorous, and therefore making smaller plants, are some of the coloured ones, such as the violet-purple 'Oriental Night'. I find it best to thin these out to intervals of no more than 100 mm (4 in) when they are sown out of doors. This annual is actually a member of the brassica (cabbage) family, and so the seedlings need to be dusted once or twice with derris dust to ward off flea beetles, a typical pest of brassicas, that could check their growth.

Candytufts (*Iberis*), with their crowded heads of flowers in white and shades of pink, are always dependable for a good show. They are sown in March or April and attain a height of about 300 mm (1 ft). Less commonly

*Candytuft (Iberis) is one of the easiest of all hardy annuals to grow, but it must be sown where it is to flower: the young plants resent root disturbance and should not be transplanted.*

*Gorgeous, hibiscus-like flowers of annual mallow (Lavatera trimestris 'Silver Cup') smother the bushy plants, which can be relied upon to bloom magnificently even in a wet summer.*

seen is the 'Giant Hyacinth Flowered White' cultivar, which grows a little taller because the flower heads are conical instead of flat. So dazzling is the white of this variety in the sunshine that the blooms remind one of silver fireworks.

At 1–1.2 m (3–4 ft) high, *Agrostemma milas* is among the tallest annuals and is very showy. The large, lilac-pink flowers are carried on wiry stems and are unharmed by rain, although they need the support of a few canes and string to keep them upright. The flowers are marked with thin, dark, broken lines that resemble machine stitching. The

plant is easy to grow and makes a good flower for cutting.

Because they look more like exotic shrubs than plants, many people would not recognise the annual mallow (*Lavatera*) as plants raised from seed to flowering in a matter of weeks. The flowers are large – up to 100 mm (4 in) across – trumpet-shaped, and very similar in apperance to hibiscus. Until recently the only colour available was a rather harsh cerise. Now there are two very attractive cultivars in 'Silver Cup', with blooms of cerise streaked with silver pink, and 'Mont Blanc', a slightly smaller, white-flowered

ground does not dry out before the seedlings have emerged.

Sowing annuals in shallow drills is far more satisfactory than scattering the seeds over a broad area, since you can hoe between the rows to keep down weeds. When the seedlings emerge, thin them out in stages, removing the weakest ones each time until they stand at intervals of about two thirds of their expected height; the rows should be similarly spaced.

Any necessary supports for taller plants must be put in place in good time. Bushy sticks of suitable length thrust into the soil between the plants while they are still quite small, so that the plants can grow up between them, is a very effective method, but such sticks are unlikely to be available except in rural areas. Alternatively you can use thin, green split-canes with string to form a mesh through which the plants can grow. Only those annuals likely to grow more than 600 mm (2 ft) tall need proper canes to hold them up. Even then it is better to arrange a mesh of supporting string or wires to contain the plants loosely rather than individual canes to support each plant. If the supports are inserted in time for the plants to grow around them naturally, the canes and wires will be well disguised, if not hidden.

The usual time for sowing hardy annuals is in April or early May, and most of them will start to flower in June or July. Some, however, are tough enough to be sown in late August or September, which results in larger and earlier flowering plants the following year. With the exception of *Anchusa*, *Mentzelia* (*Bartonia*), *Crepis*, *Dimorphotheca*, *Lavatera*, *Linum*, love-lies-bleeding, *Matthiola*, and nasturtium, all the plants I have mentioned in this chapter can be grown in this way to extend the period when annuals will provide colour in your garden. But whenever you sow them, remember that quick germination is the first vital step to success. If the soil seems to be rather dry, flood the drills with water and allow it to drain away before scattering the seeds along them.

*A mixed bed of hardy annuals is both unusual and economical to produce, yet provides plenty of interest and colour in summer.*

# Bedding
# Plants

The summer bedding plants that one buys by the boxful or in pots provide some of the most brilliant displays of flowers during those warm summer days when we spend a lot of time out of doors. Most of these bedders are what gardeners call 'half-hardy'. This means that they can be grown out of doors but are killed by frost, so it is not safe to plant them in the garden until the likelihood of frost is past. In most of southern England the last week of May is usually considered safe; farther north it pays to wait another week or 10 days before planting out.

Bedding plants are very versatile for providing colour, and need not be restricted to filling beds and borders. Planted in tubs and urns they can be used to brighten paved areas. Window boxes and wall baskets spilling over with flowers can enliven the bare surfaces of house or garage. Hanging baskets suspended from the boughs of an old tree can transform what might otherwise be a colourless area. Bedding plants are ideal fillers, too, for any spot that calls for temporary extra colour – for instance, between small newly planted shrubs.

## Planting out

As long as their few, simple needs are met, most summer bedding plants provide a long season of flowers, often starting in July and continuing until the first frost of autumn cuts them down. If they are planted out with care, bedding plants are unlikely to receive a setback and should not wilt badly. Easiest to handle are those in individual pots or compartmented containers, since they can be moved with a minimum of root disturbance. If they are grown in boxes their roots become entangled and, rather than try to pull them apart, I find it best to run a sharp knife along and across the box between the plants so that each can be lifted out with a cube of roots and soil attached.

Always water the plants an hour or two before they are planted out, a job best done in the evening. Make holes for them deep enough for the block of roots and soil to be just covered and press the earth firmly about them. Follow this by watering them in, allowing each plant about 300 ml (½ pt); then scatter slug bait over the soil. Failure to follow this simple form of pest control often results in annoying losses.

The majority of summer bedding plants sold are stocky of growth and need little, if any, staking. After planting, therefore, they call for little attention: an occasional hoeing to keep down weeds until the plants expand to fill the spaces between them; the renewal of slug bait once or twice in the early stages; and watering if the soil is becoming dry.

The quality of the individual plants you buy can have a great bearing on your success, and only the best are likely to give results worthy of your efforts. Look for short-jointed, stocky plants of good green colour. Reject any that look drawn and thin with yellowish leaves. Reject, too, any that are showing a lot of flowers: it will not matter if lobelias and, possibly, French marigolds have one or two opened flowers provided the

*Few bedding plants can outshine the snapdragons (Antirrhinum) for a bold summer display. And because they are hardier than many other bedders they cope well with the lower temperatures of a wet summer.*

*Key to plants, pages 32–3: 1 White alyssum (Lobularia maritima), 2 Phlox drummondii, 3 Cineraria (Senecio bicolor), 4 Tobacco plant (Nicotiana), 5 Pelargonium, 6 Ivy-leaved geranium (Pelargonium peltatum), 7 Petunias, 8 Pelargonium, 9 Trailing lobelia (L. erinus), 10 Petunias, 11 Fibrous-rooted begonia (B. semperflorens).*

plants look healthy and flourishing; but most other plants should not have reached flowering point, because this may be a sign that they have been starved or have become root-bound through having been kept too long in their boxes.

## Selection

Like the hardy annuals in the previous chapter, many bedding plants are best known by their popular names, and using the botanical one can be misleading. Both French and African marigolds, for instance, are forms of the genus *Tagetes*, but if you ask for tagetes you will probably be given a related but entirely different flower which goes under that name. In order to avoid confusion I have included the common and botanical names of each species.

If a complete bed or border is to be filled with bedding plants, many people use low-growing ones to provide a contrasting edge of colour, filling in the centre with a single kind or perhaps a mixture of two or three. In the small plots available in most gardens these days, there is little need for really tall plants – those that grow to a height of 600 mm (2 ft) or more – because beds are rarely large enough to warrant mass planting in three sizes. It does add a professional touch, however, if one or two taller ones are added as 'dot' plants to provide extra height and variety to the scheme.

Among those suitable for edging are white alyssum (mentioned in the previous chapter), and blue lobelia (*L. erinus*). These match each other well in height – up to about 230 mm (9 in) – and can be planted together if required. The mauve alyssum (*Lobularia*) makes a good edging on its own or in association with the white kind, though the white tends to be more vigorous in growth. There is also a colour mixture of lobelia called 'String of Pearls' that provides plants with red, purple, and white as well as blue flowers.

Other good edging plants include the dwarf French marigolds (*Tagetes patula*) in various shades of yellow and red, often with two-toned blooms, and related species of *Tagetes* in yellow, red, or orange. Both types make compact, bushy plants mostly in the 150–250 mm (6–10 in) height range. Of similar height, habit, and usefulness is ageratum (*A. houstonianum*), with clusters of fluffy-looking blue flowers, and the fibrous-rooted begonias (*B. semperflorens*), with blooms of red, pink, or white, some cultivars having bronze foliage as an added attraction. Although of a stature that makes them eligible to form an edging, all these plants can, of course, be used to fill a bed completely.

When we turn to the taller plants, those

that reach 300–450 mm (12–18 in), the choice is extremely wide, not only in the number of species but in all the various different colours and mixtures that are available. Here we find such well-loved favourites as the snapdragons (*Antirrhinum*), asters, the sunny-coloured African marigolds (*Tagetes erecta*), the sweet-smelling cherry-pie (*Heliotropium*), the quick-to-flower nemesias, the scented tobacco plant (*Nicotiana*), and the gorgeously coloured zinnias. Here, too, is the place for petunias (the cultivars with small, single trumpets stand up best to wet weather); the fiery-scarlet salvias, together with their pink- and purple-flowered forms; the bedding geraniums (*Pelargonium*) in red, pink, or white; and the gay-flowered *Phlox drummondii* and verbena, both of which produce their flowers in large clusters.

Less-commonly grown, but extremely rewarding, are the impatiens (hybrids of *I. walleriana* and *I. sultanii*), which are modern relations of the busy lizzie that used to flower pretty well the whole year round on cottage window sills. These modern cultivars grow about 300 mm (1 ft) high and have flowers in shades of red, pink, orange, and white. Unlike most other summer bedding plants they flower well in locations out of the sun and are ideal for those awkward, cool shady corners of the garden.

A most spectacular display is produced by the Livingstone daisies (once classified as *Mesembryanthemum* but now correctly termed *Dorotheanus bellediformis*). The plants form mats of fleshy stems that spread over the ground, but these are almost completely hidden when the flowers open to display their glowing petals in shades of pink, carmine, apricot, and orange. They tend to open only in the sun, however, and they close at night; but they flower so abundantly and are so colourful that one can forgive them.

Some bedding plants are noted for their foliage as well as for their flowers, and these make the best dot plants. For a tropical touch try a few Indian shot plants (*Canna*). They produce flower spikes 1–1.2 mm (3–4 ft) tall with red, pink, or yellow blooms not unlike gladioli, but they have much broader leaves. Those cultivars with bronze or purplish foliage, such as 'Dazzler' (red-flowered) and 'Tyrol' (pink), are the most striking. Equally exotic in appearance is the castor-oil plant (*Ricinus communis*), with handsome palmate foliage; again, the bronze- and purple-coloured ones stand out best.

If the major planting is low-growing, the silver-leaved cineraria (botanically a member of the genus *Senecio*), with its delicately fringed and cut leaves, provides a good contrast, as do the silver-leaved knapweed

(*Centaurea candidissima*) and *Pyrethrum ptarmicaeflorum*. The last two are both in the 300–375 mm (12–15 in) height range, while the cineraria is a little shorter.

For richness of foliage colour few plants can beat Joseph's coat (*Amaranthus tricolor* 'Splendens'), whose green leaves are brightly variegated with scarlet and yellow. It can top 600 mm (2 ft) in height in a really warm and sheltered sunny spot.

In the burning bush (*Kochia scoparia* 'Trichophylla') we have a foliage plant very different from the others. It quickly develops into a neat, oval-shaped bush, about 600 mm (2 ft) high, that remains pale green all summer. Not until the autumn does the plant live up to its name, but then it turns to brilliant scarlet and bronze. It makes an effective centre-piece to a display and can be a glorious spectacle when planted to form a low hedge along the back of a border.

**Above** *Free-flowering* Phlox drummondii *keeps up a display of brilliant flowers throughout the summer.*

**Left** *A touch of cool colour is provided by the tobacco plant (*Nicotiana alata, *syn.* N. affinis) *cultivar called 'Lime Green', but it needs careful positioning if it is not to look washed out.*

## Container-grown plants

When planting your bedders in containers you need to put in plenty of plants in order to create an impression of bountifulness as quickly as possible. Use trailing plants around the edge as well as others of at least two different heights in order to produce the greatest area of colour. Among the best plants for the edges are the trailing cultivars of lobelia, especially *L. erinus* 'Sapphire', whose deep-blue flowers have a white eye; the ivy-leaved geraniums (*Pelargonium peltatum*); pendant fuchsias with their ballerina-like flowers in many colours; and the orange-to white-flowered black-eyed susan (*Thunbergia alata*). Ordinary bedding petunias can also be most effective if you tie down their stems to the basket rim or put a wire around the top of the tub or urn; the geraniums and fuchsias should be treated the same way.

Next should come shorter plants such as dwarf French marigolds, ordinary lobelias and dwarf fibrous-rooted begonias, building up to a taller plant or two, such as some of the zonal pelargoniums (*P. × hortatum*), the upright fuchsias, the compact types of African marigold, or the cherry pie (*Heliotropium*).

There will obviously be stiff competition between these container-grown plants, so you must start off with rich soil, but one that will not dry out too quickly. For this reason it pays to use a John Innes or other proprietary potting compost. The first step with containers such as tubs and window boxes is to make sure the drainage holes in the base are clear. Cover these with pieces of broken clay pot or tile, and cover these in turn with a 25–50 mm (1–2 in) layer of coarse shingle before filling the container to within 100 mm (4 in) of the rim with firmed-down compost. Now begin planting, starting at the centre, and work more compost around the plants' roots. When you have finished there should be a space of 25–40 mm (1–1½ in) between the soil surface and the container rim to allow for watering. Wire baskets must, be lined to keep the soil in. Sphagnum moss (usually available from florists and garden shops) or polythene sheeting will do, but if you use the latter remember to make some drainage holes.

From the time they are planted all containers must be checked every day and watered whenever necessary. In hot weather they may need to be watered daily – and hanging baskets twice a day. I make a point of fixing baskets in such a way that they can be lifted down easily and soaked in a trough of water if they get too dry. Watering can be done with a can or hose, but always use a rose on the end to avoid disturbing and washing out the soil. If you start with a potting compost the plants will have plenty of food at first, but those in baskets and small urns will need feeding after six to eight weeks. The simplest way to do this is to use a liquid fertiliser that can be added to the water.

## Spring bedders

Summer bedding plants occupy the ground from late May or early June until late September. They shoud then be cleared away and the area planted with spring bedding plants, which will flower in April and May the following year. (The summer plants must be cleared at that time, even if they are still quite presentable, in order to give the spring bedding plants time to become well established before the onset of winter and to give the beds and borders a well-furnished appearance during the short days.)

The plants most commonly used as spring bedders are those of a biennial nature (though some are strictly perennials) that are easily raised from seed one year to flower early the next. These include pansies, forget-me-nots, and wallflowers, together with spring-flowering bulbs. But it is also possible to use some early-flowering hardy peren-

nials, including yellow alyssum, aubrieta, and *Phlox subulata*.

Those plants that can be raised from seed have the advantage on grounds of cheapness and the fact that they can be scrapped when the beds are finally cleared; those grown from bulbs score on grounds of convenience at planting time and reliability. Perennial plants suffer from the disadvantage that they have to be divided or propagated from cuttings and that space must be found for them elsewhere during the summer months – and this may be difficult in a small garden. Bulbs also need space for a time after the beds are cleared, but they can be replanted close together in a trench until the leaves finally wither, when the bulbs can be lifted and stored.

Raising your own biennials from seed is quite easy and takes up little more room than a row or two in a vegetable plot. Sowing is usually done in May to July, a period when the ground is often dry, so remember to flood the drills with water about half an hour before sowing. Scatter the seeds thinly – about three per 25 mm (1 in). When the seedlings appear, dust the wallflowers with derris to discourage attack by flea beetles, and keep the rows hoed.

As soon as the tiny plants are large enough to handle, thin them out first to intervals of about 75 mm (3 in) and later to 150 mm (6 in) as their leaves begin to touch. If a lot

**Below left** *Planting in a large tub. Make sure the drainage holes are clear. Cover them with pieces of broken clay pot and then a layer of coarse shingle before filling tub to about 100 mm (4 in) of the rim with compost. Gently build up compost around plant roots until compost is about 40 mm (1½ in) below rim of tub.*

**Below** *Use some trailing plants around the sides of hanging baskets to create a cascade of flowers. When watering, always use a rose on the can to avoid washing out the soil.*

*Bedding plants grown in tubs, urns, and window boxes bring life and colour to courtyards and paved areas.*

of plants are needed the thinnings can be lifted carefully and set out in a bed, spacing them 150 mm (6 in) apart and leaving at least 230 mm (9 in) between the rows to ensure that their growth is stocky. Pinch out the tips of wallflower seedlings to promote bushy growth if they show signs of making a tall centre stem. Pay particular attention to keeping the plants weed free.

Once the summer plants have been cleared and the beds prepared again, transplant the biennials into their flowering positions, keeping plenty of soil about their roots. If the ground they are growing in is dry, water the plants liberally the evening before, and again after, they are moved. If bulbs and other plants are to be mixed I find it easiest to set out the plants first and put in the bulbs afterwards; this can easily be done with the aid of a slim trowel.

Among the longest-lasting spring bedding plants are the double daisies, forms of *Bellis perennis*. They come in shades of red, pink, and white. Some cultivars, such as 'Goliath Mixed', can have huge flowers over 75 mm (3 in) across with a great ruff of petals. Others, such as 'Pomponette Pink Buttons', have dainty little button-like blooms. The plants are neat, compact, and usually about 150 mm (6 in) in height. Beware of letting them seed, however, particularly on light soils and if they are growing beside a lawn, which they will happily invade if given the chance.

Forget-me-nots (*Myosotis*) are easy to raise from seed and make a good show of blue at a time (April to June) when the predominant colour in the garden is often yellow. Height can range from about 150 mm (6 in) to 300 mm (1 ft), depending on the cultivar chosen; the shorter ones are useful for edging and combining with taller plants, the larger ones look best in a group to provide a bedding display, or they can be used as under-planting for the tallest tulip cultivars. Apart from the usual blue-flowered selections it is possible to buy seed of carmine and rose-pink forms.

The ever-popular polyanthus (*Primula vulgaris*) can be raised from seed (though not so easily as some perennials) or treated as a perennial and increased by division. During summer it appreciates moist, humus-rich soil

*Impatiens is the best bedding plant to choose for a shady spot where others would sulk for lack of sun.*

and a semi-shaded spot. For the best results from seed it should be sown under glass early in the year, then the seedlings moved into boxes and grown on in a cool frame until they are large enough to be planted out. A wide variety of different colours and mixtures is available, one of the most showy cultivars being the 'Pacific Giants' with extra-large flowers. The closely related coloured primroses can be raised in the same way.

Among the easiest spring flowers to grow are the pansies (*Viola*), which are best sown in June or July. When using an expensive $F_1$ hybrid cultivar, however, you may find that there is so little seed in the packet that it will be wise to sow it in a seed box in a frame rather than outdoors. Pansies have an extremely wide colour range and some have flowers 75 mm (3 in) or more across. But the best display is often made by those with smaller blooms, such as 'Azure Blue' and 'Golden Champion'. For the earliest display of all, choose 'Winter Flowering Mixed', which usually starts to flower in autumn and produces a few blooms off and on throughout the winter, before getting into its full stride in early spring.

Prized as much for their scent as for their colourful spring display, wallflowers (*Cheiranthus*) are best sown in May in order to get sizeable plants. Heights vary according to cultivar, but most are in the 375–450 mm (15–18 in) range, and a wide selection of individual colours as well as mixtures is available.

Although all but the shortest spring-flowering bulbs can be used in a bedding display, hyacinths and tulips are the most satisfactory. Their flowers are symmetrical, show up boldly, and look well from any angle. Hyacinths offer a colour range of light and dark blue, white, yellow, pink, and red. For massed planting in beds, bulbs of slightly smaller size than those sold for growing indoors are the most economical and just as effective, and their flowers scent the air deliciously when they open in April.

Tulips can be had in a vast range of colours, many of them attractively marked or shaded with a second colour. The time of flowering will depend on the type chosen. Early single and early double tulips bloom in April and are followed by the mid-season Mendel and Triumph divisions of cultivars in late April-May, to be succeeded in turn by the traditional Darwin and Cottage types in May. Unusual flower shapes are provided by the fringed, Parrot, and Lily-flowered tulips, which also bloom in May.

When well organised, those areas of the garden used for bedding plants are kept occupied the year round and provide a colourful show for nearly half that time.

*For summer colour, few other flowers can match bedding plants for quantity of blooms or length of flowering season.*

# Bulbous Plants

A vast range of beautiful, often exotic flowers can be grown from bulbs, corms, tubers, and rhizomes – all forms of underground plant storage organs. Most of them are happy to be moved (or stored) when dormant and when replanted will produce produce flowering plants when their cycle of growth begins again. For this reason, and because so many of them grow readily without trouble, they are some of the best-value plants that you can buy. Even anyone who has never so much as set a plant in the ground before can put most of these in almost any garden with every expectation of a successful show of flowers.

Most people think of bulbs as chiefly spring-flowering plants, but there is hardly a month in the year when one or another of them cannot be found in flower; and this is of particular importance to anyone aiming for colour all the year round. They can be broadly divided into three groups: those that are frost tender and must be lifted and stored under cover each year; a few that can be left out of doors but need a specially warm, well-drained site such as is found at the foot of a wall; and the vast majority that can be left undisturbed after they are planted, as long as they continue to flourish and flower well.

Apart from certain preferences as to site or soil, there are two important points to remember about these plants. The first is not to plant them too deep: covering them with a depth of soil equal to twice the diameter of the bulb or corm is generally enough, although you can go a little deeper on sandy soil. The second point is that their foliage must be left intact all the time it is green in order to feed and plump up the storage organ for the following season; unattractive though they may look, the leaves must *not* be removed until they have withered.

## Selection

Daffodils and narcissi (both of the genus *Narcissus*) are justifiably among the most popular of springtime bulbs. Happy in almost any soil, they thrive in most gardens, the clumps increasing in size over the years. A browse through a bulb merchant's catalogue reveals a tremendous variety of flower shapes and colours to choose from.

Hardly less popular are the gay tulips (*Tulipa*), with an even greater range of shapes and colours. Although still largely thought of as May-flowering plants, there are tulips that flower much earlier. The hybrids and varieties derived from *T. fosteriana*, for instance, bloom in early April. The water-lily tulip, *T. kaufmanniana*, together with its brilliant cultivars and hybrids, as well as the early double and early single tulips, also flower in April.

Most people are familiar with the large Dutch crocuses, whose blooms, striped with white, purple, gold, and mauve, open wide in the spring sunshine. Equally easy to grow and colourful are the winter-flowering crocuses that open in February. Their flowers are not so large, but each corm can produce six or more. *Crocus ancyrensis*, also called 'Golden Bunch', is one of the earliest. It is quickly followed by the *C. chrysanthus* hybrids and cultivars, which offer a wide choice

*Key to plants, pages 44–5: 1 Tulip (Tulipa greigii 'Red Riding Hood'), 2 Narcissus (N. 'Actaea'), 3 Narcissus (N. 'Fortune'), 4 Grape hyacinth (Muscari), 5 Daffodil (Narcissus 'Magnet'), 6 Narcissus (N. 'Cheerfulness'), 7 Daffodil (N. 'King Alfred'), 8 Mixed crocuses (Crocus).*

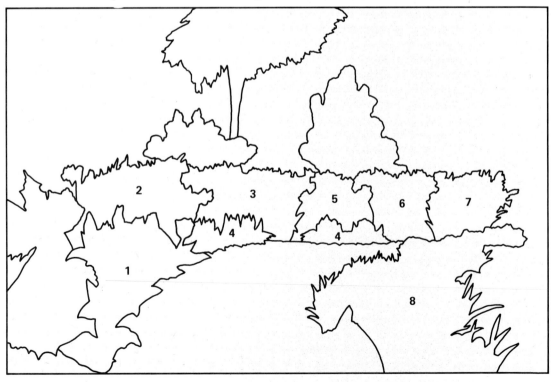

of colours, including blue; many of the flowers have petals beautifully marked or feathered on the outside with a contrasing colour. All crocuses need well-drained soil: if you plant them in clay that lies wet in winter their numbers will soon dwindle.

Less commonly seen, although readily available, are autumn crocuses and the meadow saffrons (*Colchicum*). These are no more difficult to grow, and they flower, depending on the species or cultivar, at some time in late summer or autumn, when their blue-mauve to pink and white flowers make a delightful addition to garden colour. The colchicums are rather strange in that their crocus-like flowers push up through the bare soil some time after the leaves, which appear in the spring, have died down.

A somewhat similar plant, *Sternbergia lutea*, also has large, yellow, crocus-like flowers in the autumn, but it is likely to settle down only in a sunny spot where the soil is light or has had plenty of coarse sand mixed into it, and where the drainage is very sharp, such as on a bank. It is also a plant that resents disturbance, so once the bulbs have been planted – 125 mm (5 in) is the correct depth – they are best left alone as long as they continue to flower well.

Those harbingers of spring, the snow

*Some of the most colourful winter flowers are provided by the winter aconite (*Eranthis hyemalis*). Although it is easily available this species has long been neglected by gardeners.*

drops (*Galanthus*), are among the first bulbs to flower in the year, some appearing during January in southern gardens. The common snowdrop (*G. nivalis*) has several variants, one of the best being 'S.Arnott', a vigorous cultivar with perfectly formed flowers. Somewhat later, *G. ikariae latifolius* blooms in February and March and has very broad leaves. Most snowdrops flourish in a semi-shady spot, but *G. elwesii* – a large, January-flowering species listed in most bulb catalogues – and the October-flowering *reginae-olgae*, a subspecies of *G. nivalis*, should be planted in full sun. Although usually bought as dry bulbs, snowdrops are best split up and planted while still in full leaf immediately after flowering. There are a few specialist firms who offer snowdrops 'in the green', as this is called, and it is to them you must go for the more unusual species and cultivars.

Far less commonly seen, but equally spectacular, is the winter aconite (*Eranthus hyemalis*). Its yellow flowers, each rather like a king-sized buttercup backed by a green ruff, open in January and February. The leaves follow the flowers, but die down in early summer, and the plants then lie dormant until the following winter. They are ideal for planting under deciduous shrubs and trees where the soil is densely shaded in summer but gets winter sunshine. What you buy are the underground tubers, and these should be buried in a tray of damp peat for a few days to plump them up before planting them outdoors at a depth of 25 mm (1 in).

The yellow *Iris danfordiae* and blue *I. histrioides* are two dwarf bulbous irises that help brighten the garden in February; although their stems are short the flowers may be 75 mm (3 in) or even more in diameter. These are joined before the month is out by the purple-flowered *I. reticulata*, which has rather daintier blooms. You can buy cultivars of *I. reticulata* with flowers in various shades of blue, mauve, and purple, all of which bloom at a height of 150 mm (6 in), although they are generally a week or so later in coming into flower than the type species.

In March the range expands as the glory-of-the-snow (*Chionodoxa luciliae*) opens its white-centred blue flowers. The Grecian windflower (*Anemone blanda*), which offers a choice of red as well as blue and white in its upward-looking daisy flowers, also begins to bloom then. So, too, does the Siberian squill (*Scilla sibirica*), with its dainty 100 mm (4 in) spikes of vivid, deep-blue flowers, and also its delphinium-blue cultivar, 'Spring Beauty', which grows almost twice as tall. Both carry their display well into April. The Spanish squill (*S. campanulata*) reaches its glory only in May; its spikes of bell-shaped flowers are

larger versions of the English bluebell (*S. nutans*), but they can be had in white and pink forms as well as in blue, and are about 300 mm (1 ft) tall.

April and May is the time for the easy-to-grow grape hyacinths (*Muscari*), with buds tightly clustered in a long, slim cone at the top of each stem. Most of them are blue and reach a height of 150–200 mm (6–8 in), although there is one white form (*M. botryoides album*) that is also easy to get. The common grape hyacinth is *Muscari armeniacum*, but there is now a form of it called 'Blue Spike' with double flowers that form a much thicker spike when they open.

Almost all these small winter- and spring-flowering bulbs are quite cheap and look best if they are planted in large clumps or drifts, when they can make a valuable contribution to the garden display. If planted apart in ones and twos their impact is lost. You will also find that many of them multiply readily in any well-drained soil to produce more and more flowers as the seasons pass.

Possibly the most stately of all bulbous flowers is the crown imperial (*Fritillaria imperialis*). Its large, hanging bell flowers are clustered around the top of a stout stalk some 600–900 mm (2–3 ft) high and surmounted with a tuft of green leaves. There is a number of cultivars with flowers in shades of bronze-red to orange, and also a particularly striking yellow form, 'Lutea'. The bulbs are very large and need to be planted 150–200 mm (6–8 in) deep and 300 mm (1 ft) apart in rich soil, where they can be left to develop. The flowering time is April and May, when they make a really spectacular display. But beautiful though they are, do not try to smell the flowers: the scent of many cultivars is distinctly unpleasant.

The summer snowflake (*Leucojum aestivum*) is rather like a giant snowdrop, except that the flower segments are all equal in size. Growing some 450 mm (18 in) high, the stems arch gracefully to display the green-tipped white bells in May. This plant is appreciative of a moist soil and some shade, which also helps show the blooms to best advantage.

Onions, leeks, and garlic all belong to a large genus of plants called *Allium*, which also includes a number of ornamental flowering plants that are easily grown from bulbs, given a sunny site and reasonably well-drained soil. One of the tallest is *A. giganteum*, with stout, hollow stems reaching 1.2 m (4 ft) high. The tiny violet-coloured flowers are tighly massed together to make a pompon about 100 mm (4 in) across in July. It is best sited on the sunny side of a plant that can hide most of the stem from view. *A. aflatunense* is another tall-growing species

with rather looser heads of flowers that bloom in late May. Among the brightest-coloured alliums are the yellow *A. moly*, 250 mm (10 in) tall; the white *A. neapolitanum*, 600 mm (2 ft) tall; and the pink *A. oreophilum* (syn. *A. ostrowskianum*) at only 150 mm (6 in) high. All three have much looser clusters of flowers and bloom in May or June.

Most spectacular of all the hardy alliums is *A. albopilosum*, its great heads being some 250 mm (10 in) across and made up of large, star-shaped, violet-coloured flowers with a metallic sheen that glints in the June sun. Its height varies between 300 mm (1 ft) and 600 mm (2 ft). A drawback of all the earlier

flowering alliums is that they also die down early, and once the dried seed heads (which flower-arrangers find useful) and withered leaves are removed, not only is there nothing to mark their position, but you can be left with a gap at an awkward time of year if they are planted in a prominent place.

Some of the most dainty and charming flowers are provided by the hardy miniature cyclamens. Their flowers are rosy-red to cyclamen-pink or white and are held 100–150 mm (4–6 in) above the ground; although small, they can be so abundant that there is no chance of them being overlooked. Provided you satisfy their simple needs of good

*To make a really spectacular display, spring-flowering bulbs should be planted in bold groups rather than scattered here and there.*

drainage, adequate moisture, and some shade, they will proliferate by seeding themselves. Ideal sites are between shrubs, under trees, and at the foot of a north-facing wall. There are a number of species and forms that flower at different seasons. One of the best autumn-flowering ones is the ivy-leaved cyclamen, *Cyclamen hederifolium* (syn. *C. neapolitanum*), which carries its pink flowers from August well into October. These are followed by very ornamental silver-variegated leaves, no two of which seem to be identical in shape or markings. Of the winter flowerers, *C. coum* (often sold as *C. orbiculatum* or *C. ibericum*), whose colour can vary from pink to almost crimson, and which also has highly ornamental foliage, is a delight in February and March.

Whenever possible buy your cyclamens as plants growing in pots rather than as dried tubers, which can be difficult to start into growth. If you do start with dried tubers, make sure you plant them right-side up and do not cover them with more than 40 mm (1½ in) of soil.

Summer is the time when those aristocrats of the garden, the lilies, open their beautiful flowers. Some of them are distinctly fussy about the type of soil and situation in which they will thrive, but many of the modern hybrids, such as the Mid-Century group, are perfectly happy in ordinary garden soil as long as it is laced with peat and they are well fed. Most come within the 1–1.5 m (3–5 ft) height range. Usually lilies need to be planted 100–150 mm (4–6 in) deep, and the bulbs surrounded with sharp sand to ensure good drainage, while those that send out roots from their stem bases should be mulched thickly each year with garden compost or peat in summer. An exception to deep planting is the June-flowering madonna lily (*Lilium candidum*); this often grows with its bulb tips just protruding through the soil and should never be planted more than 25 mm (1 in) below the surface.

The sword lilies (*Gladiolus*) also make an eye-catching show in summer when their spikes of trumpet flowers open. Set the corms about 100 mm (4 in) deep and surround them with sharp sand, planting them from March to May for a succession of flowers throughout the summer. Remove the old spikes as soon as they fade by cutting through the stems just above the fan of foliage; this will encourage the development of secondary spikes. The new corms are best lifted and stored in a dry, frost-proof place for the winter. The tiny cormlets, about the size of small peas, which are often produced in abundance around the new corm, can be grown on to flowering size in a season or two and provide a ready means of increase.

Late summer and autumn is the time when the tuberous-rooted dahlias are in their full glory. The range runs from miniatures to giants with flowers 300 mm (1 ft) or more across on stems 1.5–2 m (5–6 ft) high, while flower shapes can vary from neat ball-shaped pompons to the cactus types whose petals are thin and pointed. The colour range is vast, providing almost every shade except blue, and new culitivars are introduced every year. For garden decoration I find the small and medium-sized varieties are best, giving plenty of colour without entailing a lot of work in staking; the dwarf bedding cultivars need no staking at all.

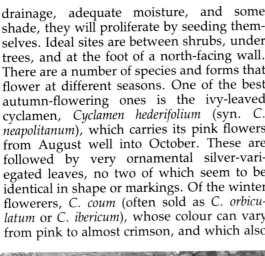

*Unlike the pot-grown cyclamen, the miniature* Cyclamen hederifolium *is perfectly hardy and flowers for many weeks in late summer and autumn.*

Dahlias can be obtained either as growing plants or as dormant tubers in spring. As they are not hardy the plants cannot be set out until danger of frosts has passed. The tubers can be started into growth in pots of soil under glass or planted out directly into the soil in May. They do well in soil enriched with garden compost or, preferably, manure. Any that grow more than 450 mm (18 in) tall must be supported by inserting three or four stout canes or stakes around each plant and surrounding it with string as it develops. Regular spraying to control greenfly, capsid bugs, and earwigs is necessary to prevent damage to shoots and flowers.

After the foliage has been blackened by frost in autumn the woody stems should be cut down close to the soil and the tubers lifted, dried, cleaned, and stored for the winter. Dividing up the tubers is an easy way to increase your stock of plants, but each tuber should have a small section of the old stem attached to it because the new shoots form only at the point where the tubers and old stem are joined.

September is the month when the flower umbels of *Nerine bowdenii*, 100–150 mm (4–6 in) across and bearing up to eight of the glistening pink trumpets, begin to open; they may carry on the display into December. Not fully hardy, the bulbs are best planted in a warm, sheltered spot, such as at the base of a south- or west-facing wall. Once established they should be left alone as long as they

*The autumn-flowering* Nerine bowdenii *is almost hardy and repays the care spent in finding a sheltered, well-drained spot for it.*

continue to multiply and flower well. Their strap-like foliage develops in spring and dies down in autumn, when the 450 mm (18 in) flowering stems appear. A group of nerines in flower can be a delightful sight, and it is well worth taking the trouble to find a place that suits them.

Also in flower in October and November are the bright scarlet kaffir lilies (*Schizostylis coccinea*). Their rhizomes are not too hardy and will be better for having the extra protection of a layer of straw or bracken over them during the winter. They make dainty flower spikes some 600 mm (2 ft) or more high and are not unlike small gladioli. There is a number of old cultivatars with red or pink flowers, but two modern ones seem to be much stronger. They are *S. coccinea* 'Major', with large red blooms, and the pink-flowering 'November Cheer'. The plants increase by means of the rhizomes and are usually sold by nurserymen rather than bulb merchants.

Finally we come to the winter-flowering Algerian iris (*I. unguicularis*, syn. *I. stylosa*),

another whose rhizomes one gets from nurserymen. This iris is hardy but, coming at any time from December to March, the exceedingly beautiful, frail, lavender-blue flowers need protection from frost. The best place for the plants is at the foot of a sunny wall, not only for the protection such a site affords but because the plants need to be kept on short commons to make them flower well. In fact it pays to grow them on what is largely a bed of rubble. Try to find, if you can, the cultivar known as 'Mrs Barnard': it has bigger blooms, and produces them more freely, than the type species.

There is no doubt that bulbous plants make a most valuable contribution to colour in the garden at every season of the year, and the majority of them are extremely reliable. But my selection by no means exhausts their potential, as the study of those fascinating spring and autumn catalogues of specialist bulb firms will bear out. Indeed, if you were restricted to the flowers of this group of plants alone, your garden could still be colourful at almost any time.

**Above** *The fragile-looking blooms of the Algerian iris (*Iris unguicularis*) open in the depths of winter.*

**Left** *The scarlet kaffir lily (*Schizostylis coccinea* 'Major') provides a brilliant touch of colour in November, when most other late plants have finished flowering.*

# Hardy
# Border Plants

One of the glories of British gardens in summer is the astonishing array of hardy border plants we can grow. Most of them are herbaceous, dying down each winter and springing up with renewed vigour the following season. It was once the practice to grow such plants together in a herbaceous border, but in today's smaller plots a bare border in winter is something to avoid. This has led to the idea of mixed planting, intermingling shrubs and other plants, including bulbs, so that interest and colour is never lacking for long from any area. If you have sufficient space, a herbaceous border will provide its own particular summer charm and will offer colour continuously from April to October as the different plants come into bloom. If you have no room for such a border, you can include some or all of the plants mentioned in this chapter in your general scheme.

### Selection

Flowering from March until May, the lungworts (*Pulmonaria*) are among the earliest of these plants; they carry spikes of blue or red blooms some 250 mm (10 in) high. *P. officinalis*, known to old gardeners as soldiers-and-sailors, Jerusalem cowslip, or spotted dog, has flowers that open blue and turn red, giving both colours together on each stalk. *P. saccharata* 'Bowles Red' is bright red from the time of opening. An added attraction of many of these plants is the white spots or markings on the leaves. Lungworts, planted in October to March, grow well in any good garden soil, but they welcome some shade.

April brings forth the bright single or double yellow flowers of the leopard's bane (*Doronicum*). There are a number of cultivars of various heights, one of the best being *D. orientale* 'Miss Mason', a single which begins flowering at around 230 mm (9 in), increasing to some 450 mm (18 in) by about two months later. This plant is sturdy and easy to grow almost anywhere. Flowering at the same time, the navelwort (*Omphalodes cappadocica*) makes mats of bright-green leaves, above which are held 150 mm (6 in) long sprays of blue flowers rather like extra large forget-me-nots. I find it valuable because it flowers on long after one would expect it to have given up, and it often produces a few flowers in the autumn as well. Its preference is for semi-shade and a soil that does not dry out in summer.

The silvery artemisias are worth growing for their decorative silver-grey, aromatic foliage, which makes an impact for most of the year. One of the brightest is a form of the southernwood (*Artemisia arbrotanum*) called 'Lambrook Silver', which can make a substantial plant up to 1 m (3 ft) high and wide. Another silver-leaved plant, the lamb's tongue (*Stachys olympica*, formerly *S. lanata*), is one for the front of a border, preferably where its lax stems of felted leaves can spill over on to a path or paving; it attains a height of 300–450 mm (12–18 in). If you do not particularly want the flowers, there is a non-flowering form called 'Silver Carpet', which stays neater for a much longer time (the

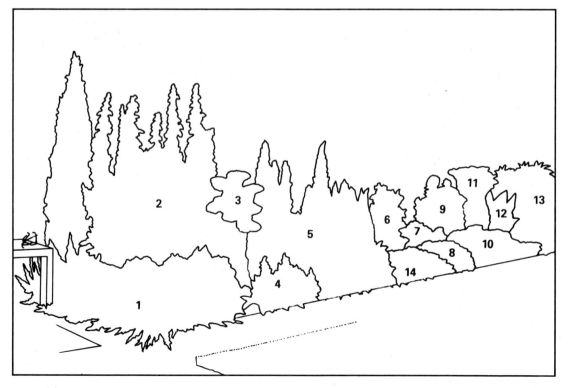

*Key to plants, pages 54–5: 1 Catmint (*Nepeta × faassenii*), 2 Larkspur (*Delphinium*), 3 Yarrow (*Achillea filipendulina*), 4 Lamb's tongue (*Stachys olympica*), 5 Russell lupins (*Lupinus*), including dwarf varieties, 6 Columbine (*Aquilegia vulgaris*, long-spurred hybrids), 7 Michaelmas daisy (*Aster*), 8 Stonecrop (*Sedum*), 9 Phlox paniculata, 10 Pink (*Dianthus*), 11 Coreopsis grandiflora, 12 Plantain lily (*Hosta*), 13 Peony (*Paeonia*).*

**Above** *Attractive in both leaf and flower, the common lungwort (*Pulmonaria officinalis*) does best in a semi-shaded spot.*

**Left** *The leopard's banes (*Doronicum*) begin flowering in April with the later daffodils (*Narcissus*), but keep going for much longer.*

flowering form tends to look a bit tatty when its pinkish summer flower-spikes fade). All such silvery foliage plants are decorative from the time their first growth appears in the early spring.

The plantain lilies (*Hosta*) are also grown chiefly for their ornamental foliage, although in some species the spikes of lilac-pink or white flowers which appear later in the season are by no means to be despised. By mid-April most have broad, or very broad, pointed leaves in different shades of green or blue-grey that may be edged or marked with bright yellow or white; the leaf surfaces may be ribbed in such a way as to appear corrugated or waved. It is not unusual to find 18 or more different plantain lilies listed in one catalogue although, confusingly, many seem to be sold under more than one name by different firms. These handsome plants thrive in shade – even under trees – yet most also do well in sun provided the soil is reasonably moist at all times.

May and June are the months when many of the best-known border plants bloom. The dazzlingly flamboyant oriental poppies (*Papaver orientale*) are joined by the multi-coloured spikes of lupins (*Lupinus*), the dainty, nodding columbines (*Aquilegia*), and the exotic blooms of the large bearded irises. The massive buds of the border peonies (*Paeonia*) that have shown promise for weeks now burst open, and the stately spires of foxgloves (*Digitalis*), delphiniums, and the blue anchusa are at their best. They are joined by the pale-yellow evening primroses (*Oenothera*), the feathery red, pink, rose-purple, cream, or white plumes of the *Astilbe* (plants that revel in a damp spot), and the scented blooms of the pinks (*Dianthus*), which are also valued for their spiky, silvery foliage. It is the time, too, when that great family of bellflowers, the campanulas, from the creeping 50 mm (2 in) high *Campanula pulla* to the 1 m (3¼ ft) *C. perscifolia*, clothe themselves in every shade from blue to purple, pink, or white, some species continuing to flower right through to September.

A splash of real gold is provided by coreopsis, best in the short modern cultivars, such as *Coreopsis grandiflora* 'Goldfink' (syn. 'Goldfinch'). Although only 250 mm (10 in) high, it blooms for several months. Equally long-flowering, one of the yarrows, *Achillea filipendulina* 'Coronation Gold', reaches almost 1 m (3¼ ft), its flat heads of button flowers being clothed with ferny foliage; another, *A. filipendulina* 'Gold Plate', grows half as high again, with massive yellow heads some 150 mm (6 in) or even more in diameter.

The fleabanes (*Erigeron*) provide colours of pink to near red or lavender to violet in their

yellow-centred flowers, which resemble Michaelmas daisies. The flowers start to open in June and, in the modern hybrid cultivars, continue for many weeks. Heights vary from 450 mm (18 in) to 600 mm (24 in), and all require staking. Some of the fleabanes with the brightest colours have names ending in 'ity', such as the light pink 'Charity' and violet-blue 'Dignity'.

The true geraniums, or crane's bills, are perfectly hardy (unlike the so-called bedding geraniums, which are actually members of the genus *Pelargonium*). All have attractive foliage and a number of them flower for a very long season, if not always flamboyantly. All are undemanding as regards soil; many obligingly flourish in shade. The tall ones tend to flop after flowering, but if they are then cut to the ground they will make a fresh crop of leaves and look respectable for the rest of the season. Among the longest in flower (from May to June) are the pale pink, 400 mm (16 in) tall *Geranium endressii*; the double lavender-blue, 250 mm (10 in) *G. grandiflorum plenum*; the rose-pink, 250 mm (10 in)

**Above** *The hardy cranes' bill (Geranium endressii) is one of the longest of the hardy border plants to flower and will thrive even in a dry, shady position under trees.*

**Left** *Modern long-spurred hybrids of columbine (Aquilegia) are showier than the old cottage-garden kinds and easily raised from seed. These are 'McKana Hybrids' of A. vulgaris.*

*G. lancastriense* 'Splendens'; and the lavender-blue, 450 mm (18 in) *G. wlassovianum.*

Few plants have been more improved by plant breeders in recent years than the day lilies (*Hemerocallis*): hybrids can now be had that bear trumpet-shaped flowers in many colours from June to August. The plants are happy in a wide range of soils; their heights vary from 450 mm (18 in) to 1 m (3¼ ft), depending on the cultivar grown, but all are tough and sturdy enough to be self-supporting. Although all these hybrids are beautiful as individuals, not every one necessarily shows up well from a distance. I particularly favour 'Golden Chimes'; its bright-yellow flowers contrast with the brown buds, and make up for their smaller than average size by their number and a flowering season as long as any.

Not to be forgotten is the catmint, *Nepeta × faassenii*. A favourite front-of-the-border plant up to 450 mm (18 in) high, it bears narrow grey leaves and sprays of mauvish flowers that open from May to September.

In July the later-flowering border plants that will carry the main display well into August and often September commence to bloom. They include the tall, white-flowered

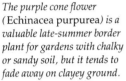

*The purple cone flower (Echinacea purpurea) is a valuable late-summer border plant for gardens with chalky or sandy soil, but it tends to fade away on clayey ground.*

*Chrysanthemum maximum.* Unless you particularly want single flowers – which are perfect, huge, white daisies – the double 'Esther Read' at 750 mm (30 in) and the slightly taller 'Wirral Supreme' will make a fine show.

*Cautleya robusta,* a member of the ginger family, can bring an exotic touch to a border at this time. Its light-green leaves are large, rather like those of the tender cannas one sees in bedding displays in public parks, but the flowers are much smaller, yellow, and carried on stiff mahogany-coloured stems. Given rich soil and moisture it can reach a height of 1.2 m (4 ft), but 1 m (3¼ ft) is more usual. In order for it to look really luxuriant I find it best to plant it where it will receive some shade for part of the day.

Light soil is the preference of the purple cone flower (*Echinacea purpurea*), which carries large rose-pink to crimson-purple blooms from July until the autumn. Although it will attain a height of 1 m (3¼ ft), it has stiff stems and can manage without support in many gardens.

The blazing star (*Liatris*) is an oddity among border plants in that its spikes of July flowers open from the top downwards, giving them a club-like shape. The 600 mm (2 ft) high 'Kobold' cultivar of *L. callilepis* is perhaps the best available, with its intense lilac-coloured flowers. Equally unusual are the bergamots or bee balms (*Monarda*), whose flowers are grouped into shaggy whorls at the shoot tips. Most commonly grown are the cultivars of *M. didyma,* such as 'Cambridge Scarlet', 'Croftway Pink', and the purple 'Prairie Night', which reach a height of 600–900 mm (2–3 ft).

Few plants can be easier to grow than purple loosestrife (*Lythrum salicaria*), a wild plant to be found in abundance beside streams in the west of England. Although it enjoys moist soil it seems to grow well enough almost anywhere given a little sun. The tall magenta flower spikes that delight the eye from July to September are usually 600–900 mm (2–3 ft) high. 'Firecandle' is a cultivar of an intense rosy-red colour, while 'Rosy Gem' is one you can easily grow from seed. If sown early in a frame, the plants will flower in their first summer. One great virtue of these plants is that despite their height they are completely self-supporting. They should be cut back in autumn.

Pride of the late-summer border are the phloxes, with their fragrant mop-heads in shades of purple to lavender, red to pink, salmon-orange, or white. Most of them grow 750–900 mm (2½–3 ft) tall, appreciate plenty of moisture and food, and flower well in sun or shade. An added advantage is that many of them are sturdy enough to be self-support-

ing unless they are growing in a very exposed position.

Knotweeds are members of the large *Polygonum* genus, many of which have red or pink flowers grouped close together in short spikes, or 'pokers'. Some of them are too rampant for a garden, but among the safe ones is the low-growing *P. affine,* which carpets the ground and is easily chopped back if it over-runs its space. The height of the June flowers is 150–250 mm (6–10 in). The best cultivar is 'Donald Lowndes', whose deep-pink pokers change to deep red by the autumn. Much larger is *P. amplexicaule,*

*A good-coloured form of the ordinary purple loosestrife (Lythrum salicaria), 'Firecandle' is a useful grow-anywhere plant.*

which can reach over 1 m (3¼ ft) in height and width in moist soils. It is very free flowering and carries masses of small, pokery flowers from July to October. The species flower colour is pink, but it is nearer red in the cultivar 'Speciosum', and crimson-scarlet in 'Firetail'. Although not flamboyant these polygonums are valuable for their long and late-flowering season as well as for the unusual shape of the blooms.

Among the plants not often seen in private gardens (perhaps because it must be increased from cuttings rather than by division), but which never fails to catch the eye of visitors in public ones, is *Salvia nemorosa* (syn. *S. × superba*) and its cultivars. It makes a mass of upright stems topped with spikes of brilliant purple flowers in July and August; and if these are promptly dead headed by cutting the stems through just below the bottom flowers, they will make a generous repeat performance in the autumn. Growing 1–1.2 m (3–4 ft) high, it seems to do well in most soils and even in semi-shade, although it does need careful staking. It has two shorter cultivars in the 450 mm (18 in) 'East Friesland' and the 750 mm (30 in) 'Lubeca', which are otherwise similar in appearance to the type species but are earlier to flower.

Anyone who has met only the old, tall, invasive golden rod (*Solidago*) should take a look at the newer garden hybrids, which are much better behaved and thoroughly garden worthy. 'Golden Shower', for instance, grows but 750 mm (30 in) high and bears arching sprays of yellow flowers, while 'Golden Thumb' at a mere 300 mm (12 in) makes a hummock of short, yellow plumes.

Moving on to August we reach the time when the Japanese anemones begin flowering. Happy in sun or shade, and in almost any soil, they sulk when moved and should be left undisturbed as long as possible. They include *Anemone japonica* (more correctly, *A. × hybrida*) and one of its parents, *A. hupehensis*. The different cultivars offer single or semi-double flowers in white and shades of pink. The most most beautiful, to me, are the whites, which show up well against a dark background. All flower on into October; the height range is about 0.6–1.2 m (2–4 ft).

Few people would recognise *Lysimachia clethroides* as a plant related to the creeping jenny or moneywort (*L. nummularia*). Although it thrives in moist soil it seems to do very well under ordinary garden conditions, rising to a height of some 900 m (3 ft). In July to September its stems are topped with white flower spikes. As these spikes develop, instead of standing up straight, as they do on most other plants, they arch over, all in the same direction, making an unusual

sight. The leaves turn an attractive orange or red in the autumn.

Among the most showy plants for late summer are the heleniums (*H. autumnale*) with flowers, in colours of bronze-red to orange and yellow, made up of wide petals around a large central knob or disc. They grow well in most soils and even the taller ones are reasonably self-supporting unless caught in a heavy storm when in full bloom. Most of them grow to around 900 mm (3 ft) high, although there are one or two, like the 600 mm (2 ft) orange-yellow 'Wyndley', that are shorter.

Stonecrops (*Sedum*) come in a great variety of shapes and sizes, but none is more attractive than *S. spectabile*, also known as the ice plant. The light-green fleshy leaves, on thick stems that grow about 450 mm (18 in) high, are attractive all summer. They are topped by large flat heads of flowers in pink or rosy red that deepen as they age from August to October and never fail to attract butterflies and bees whenever the sun shines. Taller by up to 300 mm (1 ft) is a cultivar called *S. × 'Autumn Joy'*. All the stonecrops are completely self-supporting and compact, and must rank among the top 10 border plants.

One of the latest groups of border plants to flower (in September and October) is the Michaelmas daisies (*Aster*), the most labour-saving being the dwarf varieties, such as mauve *A. novi-belgii* 'Audrey', purple-red *A. n-b.* 'Dandy', and white *A. n-b.* 'Snow Sprite', none of which is taller than 300 mm (1 ft). Other cultivars can be had in heights up to 1.2 m (4 ft) and in a very wide range of colours. These, too, are mostly derived from *A. novi-belgii*. Although the last galaxy of coloured daisy flowers in the year, they have disadvantages in that they are nothing to look at during the summer and often suffer from mildew and wilt. Mildew can be controlled by spraying with a suitable fungicide, but wilt is incurable, and if it is exceptionally troublesome your only recourse is to grow the few available cultivars of the closely related *A. novae-angliae* that are guaranteed to be completely immune to it.

Most border plants need to be lifted and split up occasionally, when they have exhausted the soil or threaten to encroach on their neighbours' territory. Use young pieces from the outer edges of the clumps for replanting. Some of these plants, however, especially the peonies and Japanese anemones, are best left alone as long as they continue to flower well. Simply scatter a little bone-meal around them and spread a 25 mm (1 in) layer of well-rotted farmyard manure, garden compost, or even peat over the soil to act as a mulch.

*Preceding two pages A well-planned border of herbaceous plants can provide colour and interest for most of the year as each flowers in its season.*

**Right** *A humus-rich soil and a somewhat shady site provide ideal conditions for the foxgloves (Digitalis).*

## Propagating Delphiniums

Delphiniums can be increased by using the young spring shoots as cuttings. Make sure to take them low enough to provide solid bases, and insert them in pots of gritty compost to root. After watering in the cuttings, prevent them from excessive wilting by covering the pot with a tent of clear polythene sheet closed at the base with an elastic band and supported by bent wires.

## Propagating Japanese Anemones

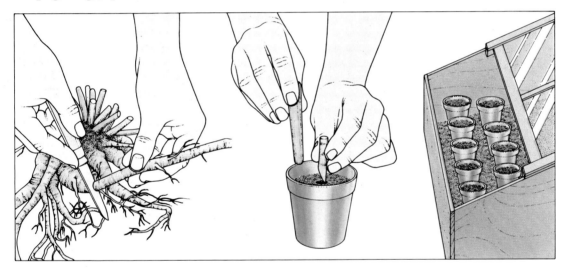

Japanese anemones can be increased with root cuttings taken in late autumn or winter. Remove a few thick roots and cut them into 50 mm (2 in) sections, making sloping cuts at the bases to indicate which way up to plant them. Plant them in small pots, just covering them with sandy compost, and put them in a cold frame. Keep the soil moist but take care not to over-water before new shoots form in spring.

## Propagating Border Phloxes

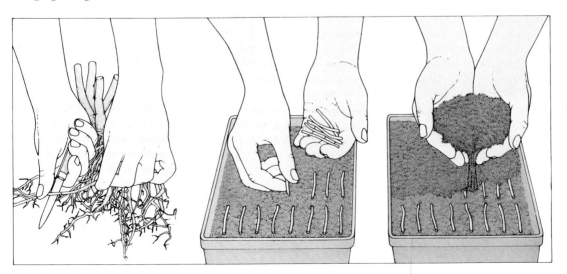

To raise phloxes from root cuttings use a sharp knife to trim the roots into lengths of 50–75 mm (2–3 in). Place them about 25 mm (1 in) apart on the surface of a tray filled with rooting compost, then cover them over with 12 mm (½ in) of the same.

## Propagation

A great many border plants are easily propagated by cuttings made from the new shoots in spring. Gather the shoots when they are about 100 mm (4 in) long, making sure in the case of delphiniums, lupins, and other hollow-stemmed plants that you sever them low enough for the stem base to be solid. Carefully trim away any leaves from the lower half of each cutting, and treat the cut end with a hormone rooting preparation. Then insert the cuttings in pots filled with a rooting compost, using a broad-based dibber to ensure that each cutting can sit firmly on the base of its hole; then gently press the compost about it. After watering the pots, cover each one with a clear polythene bag, using bent wires to hold up the plastic away from the plants and closing the bag about the pot with an elastic band. This will trap moist air about the cuttings to help prevent shrivelling before the roots form. Keep the pots in a frame, or even on the windowsill of a cool room, until they 'strike' (make roots). Light speeds root development, but direct sunlight could scorch the cuttings in their plastic tents. Once roots have formed, transfer each cutting into its own small pot. Grow them on until they are large enough to be planted out, taking care to harden them off (acclimatise them to the new conditions) beforehand in a cold frame or cloches.

A few border plants, such as anchusas, Japanese anemones, perennial blanket flower (*Gaillardia*), and oriental poppy (*Papaver orientale*), can be raised from root cuttings. These are pieces of stout root, 25–50 mm (1–2 in) long, taken in autumn or winter. They are easily obtained when plants are lifted; alternatively, just dig away the soil from one side of a plant and remove a root or two. When preparing each cutting, make a level cut across its top and a sloping one at the base, so you know which way up to plant it. Set each cutting in the compost so that its top is just covered with soil. Put the box in a cold frame and keep it damp until new growth has developed, when the young plants can be potted individually and grown on.

Border phloxes are best divided if they are healthy, but if suffering from an attack of stem eelworm they can be raised from pieces of their slender roots, some 75–100 mm (3–4 in) long and buried horizontally 25 mm (1 in) deep in a box of compost. Gently but thoroughly wash all soil from the roots beforehand in order to avoid carrying the pest over into the new medium, and be sure to use a sterilised compost and clean boxes. When planting out the new phloxes, set them in fresh garden soil or they will certainly be infested again very quickly.

If you grow plants that need supporting, position the stakes as early in the season as possible so that the plants can arrange themselves naturally and help disguise the supports. If the work is left too late, the plants tend to have a 'bundled-up' look. If twiggy sticks are obtainable the plants can be supported in the manner suggested for hardy annuals, pushing the sticks in among the developing shoots while they are still quite small so they can grow naturally through the mesh of twigs. It is more usual, however, to surround each clump with a number of canes of suitable length and to tie string around them to contain the shoots as they grow. (You can also buy proprietary brands of metal supports; although expensive, they should give years of service.) Whatever method you use, the aim of supporting is to contain the plants gently but in such a way that they cannot blow over or be weighed to the ground when heavy with flowers and rain. Do not force them to remain rigidly upright like soldiers on parade or you will destroy their natural grace.

*Flowering late in the summer, Japanese anemones (Anemone × hybrida) help to keep the display of border flowers going into autumn.*

# Ornamental Shrubs

Where would we be without ornamental shrubs to provide colour and mass in a garden? They are among the essential permanent inhabitants that go on, season after season, delighting us with their infinite variety of flowers and foliage, yet demanding little other than an occasional feed and a little pruning to keep them shapely and within bounds. Carefully chosen, they will provide colour and interest throughout the year. I have space here to mention only a few of the many hundreds of shrubs suitable for our purposes, but these will give you some idea of the forms available. The sizes given for the plants are only a rough guide since they vary considerably depending on site, soil, rainfall, and other factors.

## Selection

The barberries (*Berberis*) form an extremely various and useful genus, ranging in height from 500 mm (20 in) to 3 m (10 ft) and thriving almost anywhere so long as the soil does not become waterlogged in winter. They all flower in spring and many follow this with a showy autumn display of berries. *B. darwinii*, an evergreen, is brilliant in bloom from April, when its clusters of orange flowers open against a background of the tiny, dark-green leaves. It makes a dense bush and can reach a height of 2.5–3 m (8–10 ft) in time, but is easily kept shorter. *B.* × *rubrostilla*, which bears yellow flowers in May, is deciduous and a much smaller shrub at 1 m (3¼ ft); it is noted for its coral-red fruits, among the largest of any barberry, and ruby-tinted foliage.

The graceful arching branches of the evergreen *B.* × *stenophylla*, reaching up to 2 m (6½ ft) high, make it particularly attractive, especially when the yellow flowers open in April. More useful in a small plot is a dwarf form of it called 'Corallina Compacta', which grows a mere 300 mm (1 ft) high, with flower buds that are coral-red before they open.

A really brilliant autumn show is put on by *B. thunbergii*, when the bright-red of its berries is joined with the autumn colour of its leaves before they fall. Growing to 1.2 m (4 ft) high, its cultivar 'Atropurpurea' has rich copper-purple foliage throughout the summer, while 'Atropurpurea Nana' is even more compact at about 600 mm (2 ft) tall. All of these have orange-yellow flowers.

Buddleias are very easy-going shrubs that grow almost anywhere and enjoy plenty of sun. The ones with those long, pointed flower clusters at the end of the new shoots from July to September are cultivars of the deciduous *Buddleia davidii*. They are available in colours ranging from the very deep violet of 'Black Knight' to the pure white of 'White Cloud'. To get the best flowers, the stems, which grow every year, must be cut back hard in March or April – a treatment that will keep the plant down to a summer height of about 2.5 m (8 ft).

Less common, but most attractive, are *B. alternifolia* and *B.globosa*, both of which bear flowers on the previous year's growth. The weeping buddleia *B. alternifolia* (deciduous) has slender, arching branches clustered with scented, lavender-coloured flowers in June. It

*The pink and purple flowers of* Aubrieta *make an effective contrast to golden barberries* (Berberis) *in the spring.*

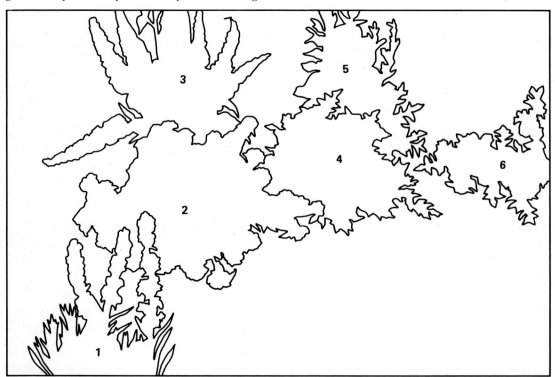

*Key to plants, pages 68–9:
1 Old English lavender
(Lavandula spica),
2 Jerusalem sage (Phlomis fruticosa), 3 Buddleia davidii, 4 Oregon grape
(Mahonia aquifolium),
5 Red-barked dogwood
(Cornus alba 'Spaethii'),
6 Shrub rose (Rosa gallica versicolor, or 'Rosa Mundi').*

*To get such an effective display of its brightly coloured young shoots, the red-barked dogwood (Cornus alba) should be cut back almost to ground level each spring. Right The foliage of this purple smoke tree (Cotinus coggygria 'Royal Purple') provides a substantial splash of garden colour all summer long.*

golden. The species is noted for the bright red bark of the young shoots; in the cultivar 'Sibirica' they are a brilliant crimson. Both must be pruned hard in the early spring to encourage the growth of young shoots, which have the brightest colouring. This treatment should keep the plants to a size of 1.5 m (5 ft) high and across.

The purple-leaved filbert (*Corylus maxima* 'Purpurea'), a deciduous shrub, has large, round, purple leaves all summer. Easy to grow, it can make a very large bush, but is easily kept to about 2.5 m (8 ft) tall and half as much across by cutting out a few of the thickest branches from the base each winter. It is especially attractive in spring, when the pinkish mauve catkins hang from its branches.

When you see a bush of the deciduous *Cotinus coggygria* (syn. *Rhus cotinus*) covered in its feathery, pink-to-grey flowers during June and July you can readily understand how it acquired the name smoke tree. The foliage is light green, with rounded leaves, and usually colours well in the autumn; the cultivar 'Royal Purple' has wine-purple foliage. Given time, smoke trees can make substantial shrubs some 3 m (10 ft) high, so allow them plenty of room.

Cotoneasters, some of which are featured in the chapter on broad-leaved trees, also include a wide range of smaller shrubs, both evergreen and deciduous. Their chief attraction is usually an autumn show of berries, while the deciduous species also have lovely autumnal foliage. They vary in form from the completely prostrate *Cotoneaster dammeri*, which creeps over the ground and is studded with bright red berries in autumn, to *C. henryanus*, which reaches 3–3.7 m (10–12 ft) high with arching shoots, large evergreen leaves, and crimson berries in winter. One of the best for a small garden is the low-growing fish-bone cotoneaster, *C. horizontalis*, which regularly carries a huge crop of small red berries, while its tiny leaves redden brilliantly before they fall. Cotoneasters are certainly among the most useful shrubs for autumn, being tolerant of almost all soils and conditions, although they flower and berry less freely in the shade.

Having scented flowers, all the daphnes are welcome, but none is more so than *Daphne mezereum* (deciduous), whose bare branches are wreathed with purple-red flowers in February before the leaves expand. Making a rather upright bush growing to about 1.2 m (4 ft), it is sometimes short-lived, although it will often seed itself if the birds can be persuaded to leave the scarlet berries alone.

One of the most handsome evergreen

is most spectacular when trained as a weeping tree about 2.5 m (8 ft) tall with an upright main stem. *B. globosa* (semi-evergreen) blooms a little earlier, when it decks itself with ball-shaped, orange-yellow flowers.

The ornamental or flowering quinces, still often called japonica or cydonia, belong to the genus *Chaenomeles*. These beautiful and easy-to-grow spring-flowering shrubs are set against a wall, more often than not, where they will thrive and flower well even in the shade; but they will grow just as happily in an open border, where they will make bushes 1.2–1.5 m (4–5 ft) high and wide. There is a large number of cultivars with a single or a semi-double bloom of white or shade of pink or red. All are beautiful in flower, one of the brightest being *C.* × *superba* 'Knap Hill Scarlet'; but it is best to visit a nursery to see them in bloom and to pick the colour that most appeals to you.

Two very fine variegated-leaved shrubs are provided by the deciduous dogwood (*Cornus alba*): in the cultivar 'Elegantissima' the variegations are white; in 'Spaethii' they are

shrubs can be had in *Elaeagnus pungens* 'Maculata' ('Aureo-Variegata'), whose pointed, oval, shiny green leaves have centres splashed with gold. Attractive all the year round, it can eventually grow into a bush about 3.7 m (12 ft) high and wide, but it is easily restrained by pruning.

April and May are the months when most brooms (*Cytissus*) are in their glory and one can forgive them their tendency to a short life span for their exuberance in flower, when they seem to create an explosion of colour. Although most are lime-tolerant, they seem to prefer a deep, free-draining, neutral or slightly acid soil. *C.* × *beanii* is a golden-flowered dwarf broom that would be at home in a rock garden, as would the creamy *C.* × *kewensis*. Both are spreading but grow no taller than 300 mm (1 ft). A little taller growing is the purple broom, *C. purpureus* 'Atropurpureus', though it too is more of a spreader. One of the most spectacular in bloom is *C.* × *praecox*, which may in time reach a stature of 2 m (6½ ft) and has cream flowers, or yellow in the case of its cultivar 'Allgold'. The tall-growing brooms with bright, often two-tone flowers are derived from common broom (*C. scoparius*) and seem to need an acid soil in order to survive for long. In commom with other brooms they need to be clipped over immediately after flowering to keep them compact. Remove most of the soft green shoots, but take care not to cut into the tough old wood.

Anyone fortunate to have a distinctly acid soil can create a heather garden. By using those plants with colourful foliage – some are brilliant yellow, others silver, bronze, or green – it is possible to create a vivid tapestry of colours that change throughout the year as each kind of plant flowers. The winter-flowering ericas, moreover, are tolerant of chalky (alkaline) soil, and *Erica carnea* (syn. *E. herbacea*) and its many cultivars seem to flourish almost anywhere, given adequate drainage and a place in the sun. They mostly grow about 230 mm (9 in) high, gradually expanding into a mat that is covered with flowers at various times between December and March. One of the earliest to bloom is *E. carnea* 'Winter Beauty' ('King George'), which opens its deep-pink flowers in December; it is closely followed by 'Springwood Pink' and 'Springwood White' in January. Much slower-growing than these, 'Vivellii' has an added attraction in its bronze-red winter foliage; its carmine flowers appear in February. Others that make an important contribution with leaf colour include 'Ann Sparkes', with deep yellow (almost orange) foliage tipped with bronze, and 'Foxhollow', a vigorous gold-leaved form.

A most welcome group of deciduous early-spring-flowering shrubs is the forsythias. All of these are glorious in flower, but best of all perhaps is *Forsythia* × *intermedia* 'Lynwood', whose branches are thickly clustered with broad-petalled, bright yellow flowers in March and April. Although stocky of growth, it can reach a height and width of some 2.5–3 m (8–10 ft), but careful pruning to remove old wood and the more vigorous shoots after flowering is over will keep it to half that size.

Except in mild areas of south-western England, the 2 m (6½ ft) evergreen tassel bush (*Garrya elliptica*) is best grown against a wall, where its foliage is less likely to be scorched by cold winds. The roundish, wavy leaves are dark green above and silvery beneath. The bush makes a subdued yet charming display in winter as its silvery green catkins gradually develop to drape the tree in January and February. Male plants have the best catkins – usually about 150 mm (6 in) long, although they may be almost double this length in really warm areas.

The Chinese witch-hazel (*Hamamelis mollis*) is an invaluable winter-flowerer: its delicate, sweet-scented clusters of strap-like, golden yellow blooms are never blighted by the weather and withstand the harshest cold in January and February. Its mid-green, felted leaves turn an attractive yellow in autumn. The plant usually develops slowly into an open, graceful shrub without pruning and, after many years, may reach a height of 2 m (6½ ft) and about as much wide. The cultivar 'Pallida' bears much paler primrose-yellow

**Above** *Being evergreen,* Elaeagnus pungens *'Maculata' enlivens the garden all year round with its colourful foliage.*

**Left** Cytissus praecox *and* C. kewensis *(inset) are two brooms noted for their exuberant display of spring blossoms.*

flowers that show up better from a distance.

Holly (*Ilex*) is an invaluable plant that can be grown as a tree, a bush, or a hedge; it can be pruned and clipped to keep it within bounds, and it need never exceed 1.5 m (5 ft) in height and can be kept quite slim. Heavy pruning will prevent it from berrying, but this is not important if you have chosen a cultivar mainly for its attractive foliage. Both the golden and the silver variegated hollies are rewarding to grow, especially for their impact in winter. *I.* × *altaclarensis* 'Golden King' is one of the best coloured forms, its almost spineless leaves being broad with a yellow margin. The 'Silver Queen' cultivar of common holly, *I. aquifolium*, has foliage broadly margined with white.

Flowering as they do from July to October, hydrangeas are worthy of a place wherever they can be grown. Their main disadvantage is that most of the many hybrids and cultivars of the common species, *Hydrangea macrophylla*, flower from buds formed on shoots that grew the year before, and these buds are susceptible to damage by frost. But provided they are not planted in frost hollows or very exposed sites inland, and get enough sun to ripen their shoots, they can be grown far from those seaside and town gardens where they are such a common spectacle. *H. macrophylla* provides two basic flower forms: the Hortensia group, with large mop-heads made up of mainly sterile florets; and the Lacecap group, with daintier flower-heads composed of a cluster of small, fertile florets surrounded by a ring of showy sterile ones. The colour of the flowers depends on the acidity or alkalinity of the soil as well as the variety. Those which are blue or purple in really acid soil are pink or red grown on an alkaline (chalky) one, while if the soil is faintly acid or neutral the colour may be neither one thing nor the other. White-flowered cultivars are white whatever the soil, but they tend to become pinkish in the sun as they age. The most reliable Hortensias include dark-blue/light-red 'Altona'; pale-blue/pink 'Europa'; deep-blue/deep-pink 'Hamburg'; violet/vivid-crimson 'Westfalen'; and white 'Mme E. Mouillière'. Those sold as indoor-flowering pot plants are rarely hardy enough to do well out of doors. Two of the best Lacecaps are the vigorous 'Bluewave', which is pink on alkaline soil, and the more compact 'Lonarth White'.

Very different from these, *H. paniculata* 'Grandiflora' flowers on the new shoots, carrying large tapering panicles of white florets, up to 200 mm (8 in) long in August and September, which gradually turn to a pinkish red as they age. It is one of the hardiest hydrangeas, and it should be pruned hard every spring to get the largest blooms. Cultivars of *H. macrophylla*, however, are best pruned as little as possible, especially in their early years. If it is necessary to thin out the bushes, do the work in spring, taking out a few of the oldest branches by cutting them off close to the ground. Removal of too much wood encourages a flush of soft growth that can be killed by frost. To give extra protection to the buds, leave the old flower heads on the bushes through the winter.

Feeding is much more important than pruning to keep hydrangeas flourishing. Give them a dressing of general fertiliser and a mulch of well-rotted manure or garden compost over their roots every spring. Few shrubs show water shortage more pitifully than hydrangeas, whose leaves and florets quickly wilt under drought stress. The more organic matter in the soil, therefore, the happier these shrubs will be. They demand generous treatment, but then they will produce a display whose beauty and longevity can be matched by few other shrubs.

*Hypericum* 'Hidcote' is deservedly one of the most popular of the St John's worts, its sunny, golden flowers opening in succession from July until autumn and making a respectable showing even in the shade. It can ultimately develop into a rounded bush some 2 m (6½ ft) high, but it will take many years to reach that size. Semi-evergreen in habit, it is reluctant to shed all its leaves except in a really harsh winter. Its creeping, low-growing cousin, *H. calycinum*, is dealt with in the chapter on ground-cover plants.

The mere mention of lavender is enough to invoke thoughts of cottage gardens, sunshine, and scent. These plants will thrive anywhere as long as they have sun and a well-drained soil. Old English lavender (*Lavandula spica*) makes a bush some 1 m (3¼ ft) high and wide, but it tends to become straggly. Much better garden plants are its modern cultivars, notably 'Hidcote', which grows 450 mm (18 in) high and wide and bears deep-purple flowers in July. (This cultivar, by the way, is sometimes listed as *L. nana atropurpurea*.) Lavenders do not make new growth from the old wood, so the only way to prune them is to cut back straggly plants hard in March or April or to trim them more lightly immediately after flowering.

Happy in those awkward, shady spots on the north side of a house or under trees, the Oregon grape (*Mahonia aquifolium*) is a most useful plant. It has evergreen, shiny, holly-like foliage, and its large clusters of bright yellow flowers on the shoot tips in March and April are followed by berries covered with a dark blue-grey bloom. Fairly slow growing, it can reach 1.5 m (5 ft) high and wide, but is

*Lacecap Hydrangea are far daintier than their mop-headed relations, but both may produce good autumn leaf colour as the season moves to an end.*

easily kept to about half this size by pruning. Somewhat taller growing, *M. japonica* flowers in January and February, when its strongly scented, pale yellow flowers open on the long trailing spikes at the ends of the branches. Given sufficient shade its evergreen foliage is a dark lustrous green, but if it is grown where it is sunny and soil is dry its leaves become bronzed, growth is much slower, and it loses its luxurious appearance.

In complete contrast is the daisy bush (*Olearia × haastii*) from New Zealand, which will not survive without free-draining soil and plenty of sun. It is the only *Olearia* hardy enough to be grown just about anywhere in Britain. Forming a rounded bush some 1.2–2 m (4–6½ ft) high, it has small, rather oval leaves that are shiny green above and white-felted below. It is smothered in yellow daisy flowers in July and August. If it becomes too straggly it can be cut back in April.

*Pernettya mucronata* is one of the most attractive of the small, berrying evergreens, but it is also a lime-hater that flourishes only on really acid soil. Usually growing about 1 m (3¼ ft) high, it gradually extends its territory by means of suckers to form a dense thicket. It will grow in quite deep shade but it will not flower or fruit so readily in such a position. The foliage is small, pointed, and dark green, and the heather-like flowers that appear in May and June are white. The large berries can be white or in shades of pink or red to near lilac, colouring up in late summer and autumn and persisting for a long time. The species is unisexual, so male and female plants must be grown together to ensure fruiting.

Many people might mistake a young Jerusalem sage (*Phlomis fruticosa*) for a border plant rather than a shrub but eventually it develops into a rounded bush about 1 m (3¼ ft) high and across. Being a member of the sage and lavender family (Labiatae), it is a contender for a place on a sunny bank or at the foot of a sunny wall. Its greyish, furry, evergreen leaves are attractive for most of the year, while the bright yellow flowers crowd in clusters around the stems in July and August – a time when many other shrubs have finished flowering.

*Pieris formosa forrestii* 'Wakehurst' must rank among the 10 most spectacular evergreen flowering shrubs in April and May, when its clusters of scented, creamy, lily-of-the-valley-like flowers contrast with the shiny, dark green old leaves and the bright red new ones. What is more, this young foliage colour is maintained for months as

*There is no need to segregate shrubs from other plants: here two shrub species, silver-leaved cotton lavender (Santolina) and true lavender (Lavandula), revel in a sunny mixed border.*

more leaves develop. It is, alas, another shrub that can be grown only in acid soil. Slow growing, its habit is to form a rather upright bush up to 2.5 m (8 ft) tall, although it may have reached little more than half that height by the end of a decade. Where space is extremely restricted but soil conditions are suitable, the more compact form *P. formosa* 'Forrest Flame' could be chosen. Its red foliage colouring is a little less brilliant, but it is said to be hardier and it is only about half the size of 'Wakehurst'. Both plants, however, appreciate shelter from north and east winds.

For sheer flower power and good, honest value, the shrubby cinquefoils (*Potentilla*) are difficult to beat. They are tough, grow-any-where plants that make tidy bushes neatly clothed to the ground, and they flower on and on in the summer. *P.* 'Elizabeth' develops into a dome-shaped bush about 1 m (3¼ ft) high and wide with light yellow flowers. *P. arbuscula* 'Beesii', at half the size, is a good front-rank plant, with golden blooms and attractive silvery foliage. A little taller at 1.2 m (4 ft) or more and with a tendency to arch, *P. fruticosa* 'Katherine Dykes' is another with pale yellow flowers, and it has deeply lobed leaves. *P. f.* 'Tanger-

*While the golden-leaved form of the red-berried elder (Sambucus racemosa 'Plumosa Aurea') is finest in spring and early summer, as here, it loses its brightness only in the autumn.*

ine', on the other hand, reaches no more than 450 mm (18 in) high, yet may spread more than twice as far. Being deciduous, the cinquefoils offer nothing for the winter season, but as most of them flower cheerfully from early June to October they deserve a place in any garden. If their growth is too exuberant they can be cut back drastically in March.

Roses are undoubtedly the most popular of all the flowering shrubs, a fact that is hardly surprising when you consider how easy-going they are and the quantity of blooms they produce even in their first season after planting. The hybrid tea and floribunda roses that offer such a variety of colours to choose from have an added advantage: the heavy pruning meted out to them allows one to site them in front of a spring-flowering shrub in the certain knowledge that after pruning they will not obscure your view of it, yet later will grow up to screen it. There is also a wide range of old species and shrub roses available that develop into distinct bushes without the need for such hard pruning. But for long-term colour you need to select repeat-flowering cultivars, such as the hybrid musk roses, in order to enjoy as long a season of blooms as possible.

Although generally thought of as a culinary herb, the common sage (*Salvia officinalis*) is a useful plant for a sunny spot; so, too are its cultivars 'Purpurascens', with purple leaves, and 'Tricolor', which has cream-splashed leaves suffused with pink and purple. Although they get straggly after some years, the plants are easily started afresh from cuttings or by layering.

The golden form of the red-berried elder (*Sambucus racemosus* 'Plumosa Aurea') is one of the finest yellow-foliaged shrubs and makes a superb show with its beautiful, deeply cut, fern-like leaves from spring to autumn. It bears yellowish white flowers in April and May and the berries follow in June and July. Prune it annually in March to keep it bushy and about 1 m (3¼ ft) high and wide. The 'Aurea-Variegata' cultivar of the related *S. nigra*, a more vigorous shrub, has green leaves with yellow margins.

A notable winter flowerer, *Viburnum × bodnantense* 'Dawn', forms an upright bush eventually some 2 m (6½ ft) or a little more high. Its clusters of scented pink flowers open on the bare shoot tips from November to March during mild spells and are completely unharmed by sharp frost.

*Weigela florida* 'Foliis Purpureis' is an admirable shrub for a small plot. Making a neat bush about 1.2 m (4 ft) high and wide, it has colourful purple-flushed foliage and its shoots are clustered with pink, bell-shaped blooms in June. Another cultivar, *W. florida*

'Variegata', is one of the very best variegated shrubs, with pale-cream-edged leaves and, again, pink bell-shaped flowers in June. A shade stronger-growing than its purple-leaved counterpart, it can make a bush about 300 mm (1 ft) taller and broader.

## Pruning and propagation

Although the amateur gardener is aware of the supreme importance of shrubs as long-term features of the garden, he sometimes hesitates to plant a particular species or cultivar because he fears it may grow too high or spread too far and so ruin the visual balance of a bed or border. In fact, most shrubs can be restricted to about two thirds of their natural size by cutting them back or thinning out the longest branches from time to time. The important thing is to know *when* to prune, and this depends on where the flowers are carried. If they are borne on shoots that grew the year before or on older wood, the best time for pruning is immediately flowering has finished; on the other hand, plants that bloom on the current year's growth should not be pruned until winter or very early spring. Although some shrubs need to be rigorously cut back, beware of over-pruning, since this tends to stimulate growth at the expense of flowering. Remember never to cut back into the old wood of brooms and lavender, which are unable to make fresh growths from the old wood.

There is hardly a garden owner who does not take an interest in propagating plants. Most shrubs can be raised from cuttings of one sort or another, but a handy method, especially with lower-growing species, is that of layering. All you need is a shoot or branch that can be bent to the ground. Make a slight cut in the bark 300 mm (1 ft) or so from the end of the branch, bend it into an 'elbow' at that point, then peg down and bury that portion, having worked some peat into the soil beforehand. Tie the upright end to a stake and keep the soil moist. Roots eventually form where the bark was cut and the branch can then be severed from the parent and transplanted. Deciduous shrubs should be layered in autumn, evergreens in autumn or spring.

Layering is a slower method than taking cuttings, but it gives a bigger plant. Most layers are ready for transplanting after one season, but there are a few notoriously slow-to-root plants, such as witch-hazel, magnolia, and rhododendrons, that will need at least two years before they are ready to be moved. Any plant that objects to root disturbance, such as clematis and wisteria, should be rooted into pots of soil or compost instead of the open ground.

*Roses come in all sizes and the miniature cultivars, especially suitable for the smallest of gardens, bloom no less lavishly than their large-flowered relations.*

# Climbing and Wall Shrubs

Walls and fences offer gardening opportunities that are not to be missed. They can provide a home for climbing and wall shrubs, while the extra protection offered by a south- or south-west facing wall enables you to try a few exotic shrubs that might otherwise fail in our climate. In smaller gardens, walls and fences have another important advantage: they allow you to exploit tall-growing plants without greatly increasing the amount of existing shade.

A few climbers, such as ivy, are self-supporting, attaching themselves to brickwork or weathered timber with special roots. Others, such as vines, produce tendrils to grab any available hold, or twine their stems around a support in the manner of honeysuckle. Yet another group thrust or scramble their way upwards through undergrowth, sometimes using curved thorns or spines to hang on to other plants, as wild brambles do in hedgerows.

Apart from those that attach themselves directly to a flat surface, the shrubs will need the support of trellis, plastic-coated mesh panels, or a series of horizontal wires fixed to a wall or fence; or the shoots can be tied to individual nails driven into appropriate points as the plants increase in height and spread.

Many climbers can be trained up vertical posts and tripods of poles – or even up an existing large tree. And if space is available a pergola (made up of pairs of vertical posts in line and connected along their tops by horizontal timbers) can make an exceedingly attractive feature when clothed with a variety of climbing plants.

There is also a large group of plants which, while not strictly climbing in habit at all, can conveniently be trained flat to give a fine display.

Some gardeners are worried that self-clingers, such as ivy or virginia creeper, will do structural damage to walls. There is some cause for anxiety if it is an old building where the bricks are bonded with lime mortar; but modern structures built with cement mortar should be safe if the building is sound, with crack-free walls. In any event, never allow plants to invade the gutters and roof.

**Selection**

Ivy (*Hedera*) is one of the most useful yet under-rated climbers; it is self-supporting, undemanding, and grows just about anywhere. Our native ivy (*H. helix*), which often appears of its own accord, has many attractive cultivars. Among the best are 'Buttercup', with bright yellow leaves when grown in sun; 'Gold Heart', whose green leaves have a central splash of gold; and 'Glacier', a small-leaved form with silver-grey foliage edged white, which is often sold as a houseplant. Variegated Persian ivy (*H. colchica* 'Dentata Variegata') is especially ornamental; it has very large leaves marked with green, grey, and yellow.

The Virginia creeper (*Parthenocissus quinquefolia*) and the Boston ivy (*P. tricuspidata* 'Veitchii'), with which it is often confused, are both self-climbing and give glorious crim-

*Key to plants, pages 82–3: 1 Honeysuckle (*Lonicera*), 2 Chinese wisteria (W. sinensis), 3 Japanese crimson glory vine (*Vitis coignetiae*).*

son autumn leaf colouring, but they do need a lot of space to romp over. Much more restrained (but also less hardy) is the Chinese Virginia creeper (*P. henryana*), another self-clinger, which should be grown in semi-shade to bring out its beautiful silver and pink leaf colouring in summer; it also has good autumn leaf colour.

Most garden hydrangeas are bushes, but a Japanese species, *Hydrangea petiolaris*, is a climber as self-clinging as ivy, with large, creamy white Lacecap flowers in June, although it usually takes at least five years from planting even to begin to think of blooming. Finer still is the related *Schizophragma integrifolia*, which behaves in the same way and looks similar to the climbing hydrangea, but flowers in July. Although both these species will grow and flower on north- and east-facing walls, their display is better if they enjoy some sun.

*Pileostegia viburnoides*, another self-clinger related to the climbing hydrangea, has two great assets: first, it is slow growing and easily accommodated on even a bungalow wall; second, it is an absolutely hardy evergreen that can be grown on a wall facing in any direction. It has rather narrow, pointed leaves up to 150 mm (6 in) long and tiny, creamy white flowers that are carried in crowded clusters to form heads some 100–150 mm (4–6 in) across in September. It is not the most spectacular of plants, but is a very useful one owing to its late flowering season and its acceptance of a shady wall.

I have put the trumpet vines (*Campsis*) last of the self-clingers because many people have been disappointed with them. It is not that they are specially difficult to grow, but they flower reliably only in a long, hot summer. For this reason they are not worth attempting away from a warm, sunny wall or in colder areas of the country. Given the right conditions, however, their effect is sensational. The best one is probably the hybrid *C. × tagliabuana* 'Madame Gallen', which produces 75 mm (3 in) salmon-red trumpets in August and September. It can be pruned hard in February or March.

Among those plants that grasp their sup-

*Both the Boston ivy (Parthenocissus tricuspidata 'Veitchii') and the closely related Chinese Virginia creeper (P. henryana) (inset) are prized for their autumn coloration.*

ports, the clematis, which hold on with their leaf stalks, are the most popular. The large-flowered forms can be had in colours of purple to blue, carmine to pink, and white. All do best when their roots are in moist, shaded ground. In addition there are a number of species which, although they have smaller flowers, carry far more of them and can be delightful. They include the May-flowering, white *Clematis montana*, and its pink-flowered cultivar 'Rubens', which has bronze-green foliage; *C. macropetala*, with double blue flowers in June and July, which also has a pink form, 'Markhamii'; and *C. tangutica*, which carries masses of little yellow blooms from July to October if it is pruned gently.

Clematis pruning is a subject that worries many gardeners, since the plants are in flower for so much of the year. The small, spring-flowering ones, such as *C. montana*, should be dealt with immediately after blooming by cutting out their flowered shoots. Large-flowered clematis that bloom mainly in May and June are dealt with in late February or March by removing all dead wood and cutting back the shoots to the first pair of plump, green buds. The other clematis – those that bloom mainly after mid-June – are also dealt with in February or March, generally by cutting all growth hard back to leave 1 m (3¼ ft) or less above soil level.

The climbing honeysuckles (*Lonicera*) are old favourites and many are worth growing for their scent alone. Among those with the brightest flowers are the early Dutch (*L. periclymenum* 'Belgica'), with purple-red and yellow flowers in May and June; and the late Dutch (*L.p.* 'Serotina'), with purple-red and creamy white flowers in July to September. The blooms of the much less common Chinese woodbine (*L. tragophylla*) expand to about 50 mm (2 in) long and 25 mm (1 in) wide across the mouth; they are bright red in bud and yellow-tipped red when open. This species is scentless, and it needs a shady site and moist soil. All the above *Lonicera* are deciduous. Of the evergreen forms, grown for their foliage, one of the best is the Japanese honeysuckle (*L. japonica* 'Aureo-reticulata'), whose leaves are netted with bright gold. Its fragrant white or pale-yellow flowers bloom from June to October.

Another twining climber grown for its foliage is the deciduous Kolomikta vine (*Actinidia kolomikta*). The young leaves are purplish at first, turning to green, but many develop bright white and pink variegation over part of their surface. It seems that warmth brings out this colouring, so the plant is best sited against a south or west wall

in full sun. One could not claim that it makes a bright display (its small white flowers appear in June), but I find it pleasing and it is certainly unusual. This is not a vigorous climber, usually reaching no higher than 3.7 m (12 ft). A word of warning: the plant seems to hold some special fascination for cats, so if you plant one, give it anti-cat protection while it is young.

One of the fastest-growing deciduous climbers, the Russian vine (*Polygonum baldschuanicum*) – also known as the mile-a-minute vine – is just the thing for covering a garden eyesore quickly. It is rampant, adding as much as 4.5 m (15 ft) in a year, but it is very handsome when covered with its long, pinkish plumes of flowers in July to September; the flowers darken as the fruits ripen, maintaining a display until October. The related *P. aubertii* closely resembles the commoner Russian form, and is I think more attractive, having white or greenish plumes until the fruits begin to ripen.

**Above** *Flowers of the early woodbine or Dutch honeysuckle (*Lonicera periclymenum *'Belgica') are fragrant as well as colourful.*

**Left** *Clematis macropetala makes up for the smaller size of its flowers by the profusion with which they grow.*

*The Chinese wisteria (Wisteria sinensis) is a very long-lived plant. Fragrant swags of the lovely mauve flowers festoon its branches each May.*

**Right** *Two of the best ornamental vines are the 'Purpurea' and (inset) the 'Brandt' cultivars of the grape vine (Vitis vinifera).*

which you will easily recognise from their clusters of flowers. The Chinese potato tree (*S. crispum*), best in the form of its cultivar 'Glasnevin' (syn. 'Autumnale') has flowers of a rich blue with a yellow centre that open in sequence throughout the summer. Hardier than the type species, it may be killed to the ground by frost, but it will spring up again the following season. If the top growth is not killed, however, it may start to bloom as early as May. 'Glasnevin' is better described as a scrambler than as a climber: you will need to support its new-season shoots. The other recommended member of this genus is the jasmine nightshade (*S. jasminoides* 'Album'), a robust twiner that can put on 3.7 m (12 ft) of growth in a season, but is slightly more tender and liable to be cut by frost. It too carries its flowers, which are white, all summer long. Both have the advantage of flowering well in their first season from planting.

The deservedly popular Chinese wisteria (*Wisteria sinensis*), with its long hanging clusters of mauve pea-flowers, makes a delightful display in May and June. Having even longer flower racemes, the show put on by *W. floribunda* 'Macrobotrys', a form of the Japanese wisteria, can be breathtaking when trained to an arch or pergola. Both these twiners will climb any suitable support, but like the honeysuckles they should not be put on a tree or a shrub or they may eventually strangle its branches.

Roses are, perhaps, the most popular of the non-self-supporting climbers. They are not the best plants for a hot, sunny wall (where one so often sees them) because they almost inevitably suffer from mildew there. In any case, I think that such a favoured site is better reserved for something more unusual. Roses can be grown on pergolas, up pillars, or fanned out on a fence or trellis screen. Most suitable for pillars, I find, are the ramblers, since most if not all the old shoots are removed at pruning time and the new ones can be spiralled around the support. There are so many roses available that it is mostly a matter of picking the colour your prefer.

Although usually seen growing against a wall, the winter-flowering jasmine (*Jasminum nudiflorum*) is perfectly hardy and can be grown as a shrub in the open. It makes a spectacular sight, however, if it is neatly trained to a flat surface; the young shoots arch from it and are bejewelled with yellow flowers from November to March. Hard frosts may kill the open blooms, but they are quickly replaced by the unharmed buds. This is certainly one of the most valuable of all winter-flowering shrubs for colour.

One or two true vines make very attractive climbers. Perhaps the most spectacular is *Vitis coignetiae*, with its huge leaves, as much as 300 mm (1 ft) across, that are green above and rusty brown below, and turn brilliant shades of red in autumn. The species is, however, too vigorous for anything less than a lofty tree or large house. Of more modest habit is the grape vine, *Vitis vinifera*. One of its cultivars, 'Purpurea', has foliage that turns purple in summer; another, 'Brandt', makes a superb show of autumn colour (orange, crimson, and pink) and also provides grapes good enough to eat in a warm year if it is grown against a wall.

If you have space available along a sunny wall, two of the best-value flowerers are members of the potato family (*Solanum*),

Common jasmine (*J. officinale*) carries clusters of white, deliciously scented flowers at its shoot tips from June to September. Unlike its winter-flowering cousin it is a vigorous-growing twiner and needs the protection of a sheltered corner in really cold districts. The best form to buy is 'Affine', which has slightly larger, more numerous flowers that are usually tinged with pink on the outside. Although it can be trained over a support, it usually looks better if it is allowed to scramble naturally among trees and shrubs.

Another yellow flowerer, the Jew's mallow (*Kerria japonica*), produces long, arching, green-barked stems that can be fanned out against a fence or shed. Its best-known cultivar, 'Pleniflora' ('Flore Pleno'), has double orange-yellow flowers that are more attractive than the single blooms of the type species. Again, these plants are not strictly climbers. Height is normally about 2 m (6½ ft), but can be more against a wall. The blooms appear in April and May at the ends of the previous season's shoots.

Perhaps the most spectacular of all wall shrubs is the magnificent evergreen *Magnolia grandiflora*. Its huge bowl-shaped, creamy white flowers open sporadically from July until the cold October weather puts paid to any remaining unopened buds. Anyone who has seen and smelled these gorgeous blooms on a tree or stretching up for perhaps three storeys on an old building probably imagines that such a delight would be beyond the scope of someone with a modest-sized house. And if you had a young plant of the ordinary species you would probably be right; indeed, you could easily wait 30 years or more to see a flower at all. But if you buy a plant of the 'Exmouth' form, or possibly better still one of 'Goliath', it could be flowering within five years and be no more than 1.5 m (5 ft) high. In common with all magnolias the plants should be set out in May, working plenty of peat into the soil beforehand and packing more around the roots at planting time. Magnolias are an exception to the very-firm-planting rule since their fleshy roots are easily damaged. Being evergreen, the cultivars mentioned need some shelter to protect the attractive, glossy foliage from wind damage; their flowering performance will be enhanced if they get plenty of sun to ripen the new growth each year.

Other common shrubs which can be trained up supports include the flowering quince (*Chaenomeles*) and *Garrya elliptica* (already mentioned in the previous chapter); *Forsythia suspensa*; the firethorns (*Pyracantha*), which carry hugh crops of red, orange, or yellow autumn berries; and the decorative brambles (*Rubus*). All are easy to grow.

*Young growth on a weeping willow (*Salix*) and a magnolia in full bloom combine with an underplanting of heathers (*Erica*) to make a colourful picture in the spring.*

# Ground Cover

Every new gardener soon discovers that any soil he leaves bare will quickly be invaded by plants. Some of these may be the children of self-seeding plants he is growing nearby, but more often they will be weeds. If you look under a thick shrub whose branches sweep the ground you will find few if any weeds. Weed seedlings, like any other plant, need light in order to grow: deny them light and they will quickly die. Hence the value of what are known as ground-cover plants.

Any plant, large or small, that effectively shades an area of soil around it for most of the year is a prospective candidate, and many are now valued specifically for their ground-covering abilities. It is the modern way to reduce time needed for garden maintenance. It can also be a most colourful way, especially if low-growing plants are used as ground cover under and around trees and larger shrubs, or over bulbs which will grow through them to the light. But it is not a miracle method: ground-cover plants will not kill off established weeds like couch-grass and ground elder. The first step, therefore, is to dig and weed the area thoroughly, or treat it with a complete herbicide. For the first season or two after planting you must also hoe and hand weed around the plants until they grow together. Thereafter, however, there will be very little weeding to be done.

Many of the bushy and prostrate conifers are expert ground coverers, as are shrubs such as *Erica carnea*, *Berberis thunbergii*, the ivies (*Hedera*), *Mahonia aquifolium*, and *Pernettya mucronata*, which have been dealt with elsewhere. Good border plants for this purpose include the lungworts (*Pulmonaria*), the navelwort (*Omphalodes cappadocica*), garden pinks (*Dianthus*), hardy geraniums, day lilies (*Hemerocallis*), catmint (*Nepeta*), ice plant (*Sedum*), and knotweeds (*Polygonum*), which have been described in Chapter 5.

A surprising number of rock plants excel as ground-cover plants. I do not mean the true alpines, which need a specially prepared site with perfect drainage, but old favourites such as yellow alyssum, white arabis, some of the thrifts (*Armeria*), rock cress (*Aubrieta*) in its various hues from purple to pink, some of the delightful rock phloxes, the rose-pink *Saponaria ocymoides* (easily raised from seed), as well as many saxifrages and sedums. Given reasonable drainage and a place in the sun they will spread themselves on the flat and make a carpet of colour in their season.

Of special importance are those plants that do not insist on a lot of sun in order to flower, or that have coloured foliage. These are the ones that can be grown under and between shrubs and around taller plants. Some of them are well known, like the lily-of-the-valley (*Convallaria*), whose scented bells appear in spring, and the June-flowering London pride (*Saxifraga umbrosa*), which makes neat, close-packed rosettes of leaves and bears dainty spires of tiny pink flowers in June. Lady's mantle (*Alchemilla mollis*) is a grow-anywhere plant admirably suited to the front of a border. Its soft, pale-greyish green leaves appear pleated at first before opening up into their rounded shape. The tiny sul-

**Right above** *Colourful creeping thymes* (Thymus) *are ideal paving plants since they do not mind being stepped on occasionally.*

**Right below** *Happy in the shade of trees, the navelwort (*Omphalodes cappadocica) *flowers for week after week in the spring.*

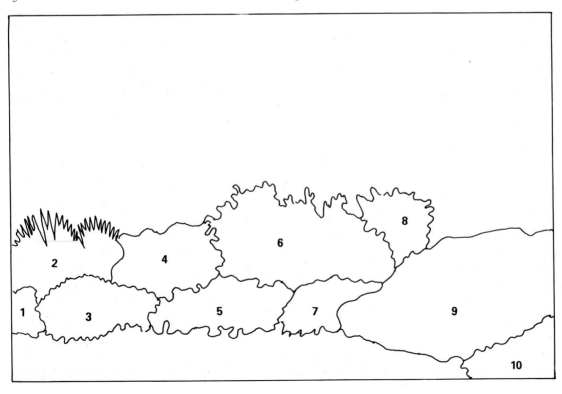

*Key to plants, pages 92–3:*
*1 Bugle (* Ajuga reptans)*, 2 Festuca glauca, 3 Marjoram (*Origanum vulgare)*,*
*4 Perennial candytuft (* Iberis sempervirens)*,*
*5 Waldsteinia ternata,*
*6 Periwinkle (* Vinca)*, 7 Thrift (* Armeria)*, 8 Yellow alyssum (* Alyssum)*, 9 Rue (* Ruta graveolens)*, 10 Rock cress (* Aubrieta)*.*

phur-yellow flowers are borne in loose sprays above the foliage from June to August. Although somewhat subdued in its colouring, it makes an excellent 'contrast' plant in sun or partial shade. Its leaf height is about 300 mm (1 ft), with flower stems nearly double this.

A lighter touch is provided by the pearl everlasting (*Anaphalis triplinervis*), with its oval, pointed, grey leaves and tiny white 'everlasting' flowers that bloom for up to three months in summer. It grows about 230 mm (9 in) tall, is partial to moist soil, but must have an open position with plenty of light, where it quickly makes large clumps.

It is hardly surprising that the large, rounded, shiny, leathery leaves of bergenias (members of the saxifrage family) led to these plants being called elephant's ears. *Bergenia cordifolia* and its cultivars and hybrids are essentially evergreen except in the worst of winters. Usually deep green in colour, the foliage of some bergenias changes to bronze or maroon in the winter. The flowering season is early to late spring, according to

*The coloured cultivars of creeping bugle (Ajuga), like this one called 'Burgundy Glow', provide an attractive mat of leaves in the shade of trees and shrubs.*

prettiest are *E.* × *versicolor* 'Sulphureum', which has coppery coloured young foliage in spring and pendulous, pale-yellow flowers, and the Japanese *E.* × *youngianum* 'Niveum', with bronze foliage and showy white blooms. Most of these plants grow 230–300 mm (9–12 in) tall, although their flower sprays may be considerably taller.

Happy in sun or partial shade, the alum roots (*Heuchera*) are as good around shrubs as in a front-of-the-border spot. The most common species is *H. sanguinea*, a hardy perennial which is easily raised from seed, although the colour of the seed-grown plants is not always true to the rosy red of the parents. You can buy a number of named cultivars, however, with flowers from scarlet, through purple-red and pink, to white. The plants form clumps of rounded leaves some 200 mm (8 in) high. The long dainty stems of the tiny trumpet flowers are more than twice as tall and put on a display for months from June; they make good cut flowers, too. *Heucherella*, a cross between *Heuchera* and a related *Tiarella* species, is a similar plant but somewhat larger and more vigorous. Its cultivar 'Bridget Bloom' carries a profusion of light-pink flowers in spring and often gives a second show in late summer.

The rose of sharon (*Hypericum calycinum*), one of the St John's worts, spreads horizontally by means of stolons (prostrate creeping stems) and is an excellent ground coverer, especially on a bank. The large golden blooms, each up to 75 mm (3 in) across, with a central ruff of stamens, flower from June to September; although the plant grows happily in shade it flowers well only in the sun. It is an evergreen by inclination and the old foliage is best sheared off in early spring before the new growth appears. The rose of sharon's method of spread makes it a highly competitive shrub that is inclined to invade the territory of low-growing neighbours – even a well-established lawn – so be careful where you plant it.

Few plants can surpass the perennial candytuft (*Iberis sempervirens*) 'Snowflake' as a ground coverer. It spreads gently by means of underground stems to form a dense mat some 230 mm (9 in) high and as much as 1 m (3¼ ft) across. Its dark, evergreen foliage is effective all the year round and the plants are smothered in dazzlingly white flowerheads in May. Apart from being a few inches shorter, the cultivar 'Little Gem' is very similar. Both can be increased by means of cuttings or by careful division. It is sometimes suggested that these plants should be grown in sun, but I once grew 'Snowflake' for many years in a rather shady spot, where it continued to thrive and flower well.

type, when clusters of carmine to pink or white blooms, usually bell-shaped, open on thick stalks. Foliage height is usually 200–300 mm (8–12 in), but is a little less in some of the modern hybrids.

Among plants that are less commonly grown, although they are not so rare as they once were, are the various coloured-leaved forms of the common blue bugle (*Ajuga reptans*) such as grey-green and white 'Variegata'; 'Multicolor' ('Rainbow'), with leaves that are mottled with yellow and flushed with pink; and 'Burgundy Glow', whose foliage is tinted with shades of wine red. All are easy to grow in moist soil and develop the best foliage in light shade. Their spires of blue flowers appear from April to June, but often have a second showing in late summer.

Perhaps at their best when growing in light shade, the barrenworts (*Epimedium*) spread slowly to make a carpet of dainty evergreen foliage topped with sprays of mostly yellow, red, or pink flowers in mid-spring to early summer. There are several species and hybrids that are garden-worthy. Among the

Creeping jenny, or moneywort, is often to be found in rock-plant lists under its botanical name of *Lysimachia nummularia*. It is a vigorous evergreen creeping plant that grows almost anywhere in moist soil. Its prostrate stems are lined on either side with small, round, bright-green leaves; golden, buttercup-like flowers open along these leafy chains in June and July. Equally easy to grow is its golden-leaved cultivar, 'Aurea', which, although a little less quick-growing, makes a wonderful splash of colour from spring to autumn. In winter the leaves turn to a very light brown colour.

Few foliage plants can outshine the gold-leaved form of our native herb marjoram (*Origanum vulgare* 'Aureum'). Its leaf colour is brilliant and when viewed from a distance is frequently mistaken for a patch of flowers. Reaching a height of some 230 mm (9 in), it produces magnificent clumps that remain vivid for most of the year. Its tiny, hardly noticeable purple flowers bloom in July and August.

One of the best evergreen ground coverers for shady areas, *Pachysandra terminalis*, has toothed, shiny leaves of rich green that give a luxuriant appearance to the area. It carries dainty spikes of white, scented flowers in early spring. Happy in acid to neutral soil, it steadily increases its area of influence by means of underground stems, creating a 250 mm (10 in) thick mat of growth. It will happily swamp low-growing neighbours, but it cannot harm larger shrubs and trees. 'Variegata' is a silver variegated form that I find more attractive than the type species.

A plant I value for the contrast its ferny foliage can make with other plants is rue (*Ruta graveolens*). The colour of the species leaves is grey-green, but in its cultivar 'Jackman's Blue' they are blue-grey and very striking. The height and width of the plants is about 450 mm (18 in). These rues are evergreen and prefer a place in the sun, but provided the soil is well drained they do not seem to mind whether it is light or heavy. It pays to cut back the plants in spring to help keep them bushy.

Another attractive evergreen lover of shade

*Although slow to increase, the barrenworts (Epimedium) eventually create dense ground cover. The ivory white flowers of this cultivar (E. × youngianum 'Niveum') show up particularly well.*

is *Tiarella cordifolia*, one of the foam flowers. (page 101). Its foliage creates a 100 mm (4 in) high carpet that is green in summer and tinged with bronze in winter. In May and June the plants carry feathery plumes of white flowers above the leaves. Given a moist, peat-enriched soil in the shade of shrubs it can spread quickly – not to say rampantly – but it is certainly one of the prettiest shade flowers. *T. wherryi* enjoys the same conditions, but is clump-forming, slow-developing, and therefore a less efficient ground coverer. It may, however, be a better choice for a very small garden. The flower plumes of this species are pinkish white.

Among the most useful and best-loved of all ground-covering plants are the peri-winkles (*Vinca*), which grow and flower in both shade and full sun. If you have space to cope with it the variegated form of the greater periwinkle (*V. major* 'Variegata') is the best. Its foliage is well marked with creamy-white and shines out even in a dull spot. The wandering shoots can be several feet long, however, and will scramble over the soil as they lengthen, eventually rooting at their tips. In very small plots, therefore, a better choice is the lesser periwinkle (*V. minor*) in one or other of its several cultivars, which offer leaves variegated with yellow or white as well as both single and double flowers in plum purple, blue, or white. Reaching some 200 mm (8 in) high, they do creep, but slowly, and are easily kept under control. Their main flowering time is April to June, but you will find that odd flowers open any time from then until the autumn. Although periwinkles are shrubs, when large enough they can be lifted, divided up, and replanted like border plants at any time between September and April.

Presumably on account of its size (I cannot think of any other reason) *Waldsteinia ternata* is usually listed under rock plants or even alpines. Yet it is a very versatile plant, flourishing in sun or shade, in dry soil or moist. It produces an evergreen mat, some 100 cm (4 in) high, of dark-green leaves which somewhat resemble those of the strawberry, but are smaller. It is a very well mannered plant, spreading but not rampant, and bears sprays of bright-yellow flowers in spring.

Some of the ornamental grasses are also useful ground-cover plants and add colour for many months of the year. I particularly like the old gardener's garters (*Phalaris arundinacea* 'Picta'). It grows well on any soil from sand to clay and, although more luxuriant of growth where the soil is moist, copes very well if it tends to dry out during the summer. What is more it does not mind being planted in a spot shaded by a wall or fence. It is a

*As well as keeping down weeds, ground-cover plants soften the hard straight lines of a path or paving if allowed to sprawl over the edges.*

*An underplanting of
Anemone ranunculoides
and* Aubrieta *here set off the
delightful spring-flowering
Magnolia stellata.*

graceful plant that can reach 1 m (3¼ ft) in height, with stout stalks and white-striped leaves, and is eventually topped with feathery flower plumes. It is not an evergreen, but the dried stems and leaves remain attractive for most of the winter and can be left in place until new growth is due in early spring.

Much shorter at 150 mm (6 in) tall, although the flowering stems can be almost twice that height, *Festuca glauca* makes neat clumps of bright blue-grey that are as useful for edging as they are planted in bold groups, and provides an interesting contrast with broad-leaved plants. *F. eskia* is a dark green species that also makes dense ground cover. Both these need a sunny site and well drained soil. Bowles golden grass (*Milium effusum* 'Aureum'), on the other hand, is

happier in cool soil and shade, where small plants soon make solid clumps. It is particularly effective in spring, when its colour is bright gold. This grass will cast a little seed about, but as all its progeny are golden, too, this is no real disadvantage.

There is no mistaking the relationship of the 300 mm (1 ft) tall *Lamium maculatum* with the common dead-nettles, owing to the shape and form of its foliage and pink flowers. Its dark green leaves, each with a broad centre stripe of silver, make an interesting display throughout spring and summer. Most striking of all is its cultivar 'Beacon Silver', in which the silver area covers almost the entire leaf surface. Having bright yellow leaves, but still with the silver stripe. *L.m.* 'Aureum' stands out well, but is rather slow growing. Both the species plant and the cultivars thrive best in shade and humus-rich soil that does not dry out. Given these conditions they quickly spread to make large mats of growth. Unfortunately, slugs enjoy both these conditions and the plants as well, so slug bait is called for every spring.

The related yellow archangel (*L. galeobdolon* 'Variegatum') is a much more vigorous plant. It has very attractive small silver-marked leaves, but it sends out long trails that rapidly march across the ground and even up among the branches of low-growing shrubs. It is ideal for growing beneath trees, where it will settle down to provide a handsome mat 250 mm (10 in) high, but it is not safe to plant elsewhere unless you are prepared to curb its invasive tendencies.

By careful selection and siting, ground-cover plants eventually create a living carpet of green, grey, silver, yellow, red, and purple foliage that is effective in most cases the whole year round; their flowers can be regarded as a delightful bonus. Most of these plants should be planted about 300 mm (1 ft) apart to give quick coverage, and this entails using a lot of plants. However, since most of them root as they spread or make vigorous clumps, they can be divided up every season or two to make more of them until you have sufficient for all your needs. You cannot do this with any of the conifers or with most of the shrubs you use for this purpose, but these do not in any case need to be planted so close together.

**Above** *Being an evergreen, the foam flower (*Tiarella cordifolia*) is ideal for ground-cover. Its foliage has bronze tints in winter.*

**Left** *All the dead-nettles (*Lamium*) need some shade to produce a good show of foliage. None is more spectacular than 'Beacon Silver', whose leaves are covered with a silvery tinge.*

# Hedges

A hedge can be one of the most prominent features of a garden, yet few amateur gardeners seem to appreciate the great variety of hedging plants that is available or give much thought to which of many possible roles their hedges are intended to play. A hedge can mark a boundary or be used to divide a garden into separate areas. If it is reasonably dense and high it will offer not only privacy but shelter from wind – or a screen to hide a compost heap, dustbins, or other potential eyesores. It can act as a backdrop to beds and borders or, more interestingly, it can provide colour in its own right by way of flowers, foliage, and berries. For these and other reasons, then, you should have a pretty clear idea of the overall design of your garden, including the larger permanent plantings, before you decide which hedging plants to use. For example, if the main area in front of a hedge will be put down to grass, it would be a pity to plant the kind of hedge that will also be permanently green. On the other hand, a hedge in full flower is likely to be merely distracting if it is sited immediately behind border plants in bloom.

If you have a small garden, of course, you must decide first if you have enough space to accommodate a hedge at all, rather than a fence or a wall; your hedging plant must either have an essentially vertical habit of growth or stand being clipped to prevent it encroaching too far into the garden. Only a large garden can comfortably accommodate a lax, informal screen; and, incidentally, a tall screen that looked impressive in a large plot might well be claustrophobic in a small one. Speed of growth may be important if you have a new garden and need to provide a screen as quickly as possible; but remember that quick growth will involve you in more frequent clipping once the screen has reached the required size. You will save yourself a great deal of labour in the future if you are prepared to wait three or four seasons for your hedge to develop, rather than insist on maximum vigour of growth in the early stages. Some of the traditional hedging plants, such as holly and box, are not as slow-growing as many people believe (though yew, perhaps the finest of all, *is* very slow – and very expensive). As long as you prepare the site properly before planting and help the plants to become established, they will soon make a handsome screen.

Preparation of the site involves digging a trench about 900 mm (3 ft) wide and 600 mm (2 ft) deep where the hedge is to be sited and working in plenty of well-rotted manure or garden compost. If neither of these is available, use leaf mould or peat instead, and fork a dressing of general fertiliser into the soil to provide food for the young plants. Be sure to buy only plants that are bushy and short-jointed and have roots that are firm and moist. Deciduous species should be planted in the dormant period between October and March in ground prepared up to six months before; evergreens are planted in April or May in ground prepared the previous autumn. The first clipping should not be made until at least a year after planting.

*Key to plants, pages 102–3:*
*1 Barberry (Berberis),*
*2 Floribunda rose 'Queen Elizabeth', 3 Beech (Fagus).*

## Selection

The commonest garden hedging plant is green privet (*Ligustrum ovalifolium*), miles of which can be seen bordering suburban plots all over the country. Its main virtue is cheapness, but it has two serious disadvantages if used extensively: it is a very hungry plant, tending to impoverish the surrounding soil, and it needs frequent clipping. Another plant commonly used for short hedges is the small-leaved Japanese honeysuckle (*Lonicera nitida*). For tall screens the most frequently used are Lawson's cypress (*Chamaecyparis lawsoniana*) and much-faster-growing Leyland cypress (*Cupressocyparis × leylandii*). All these evergreens retain their colour throughout the year: although they provide an excellent background to flowers in summer, they make a rather monotonous contribution to garden colour in other seasons. Make a point, then, of choosing coloured-leaved cultivars to add variety to the scene. If you wish to use privet, for instance, the golden form (*L. ovalifolium* 'Aureum') will do much to brighten an otherwise cheerless, open site, especially in winter; be warned, however, that it may shed its leaves in severe winters if it is in an exposed position. The Japanese honeysuckle also has a beautiful golden form (*L. nitida* 'Baggesen's Gold'); it is, however, much more expensive that the golden privet and rather slow growing.

Some of the best hedging plants are provided by the conifers, including the various forms of Lawson's cypress mentioned in Chapter 12. The western red cedar (*Thuja plicata*) can be clipped to shape in August and makes a fine bright-green hedge, especially on chalk soils. It also has the advantage of being able to make new growth from old wood if it has to be cut back severely. Yew (*Taxus baccata*), in spite of its leisurely growth rate, can sometimes be encouraged to put on 150 mm (6 in) a year if it is kept well fed.

The common laurel (*Prunus laurocerasus*) makes a fine hedge; its popularity, which waned after Victorian times, is now increasing as people rediscover its virtues. Few other evergreens grow as well in shade as the laurel, or put up so well with drips from

*Beech (*Fagus*), whether the green or the copper variety shown here, is easily clipped to make a fine hedge that holds its russet foliage (inset) throughout winter.*

overhanging trees. Its polished leaves are good reflectors, sparkling with yellow in sunlight, and echoing the blue of a clear sky on the shady side. One of its best cultivars for hedging is called 'Rotundifolia'.

A rich colour can be provided by the related sand cherry (P. × cistena). It is deciduous, but its small crimson-purple leaves make a delightful show from spring to autumn; as a bonus it bears white flowers in March and April. Of modest growth-rate, in mature form it can be clipped to make a neat hedge of about 1.2 m (4 ft) or less.

Among several hollies, the best hedging ones are cultivars of Highclere holly (Ilex × altaclarensis), which are virtually thornless. One of the most decorative is 'Lawsoniana', whose dark green leaves are splashed with yellow. It bears orange-red berries throughout the winter. If possible choose an open site – the leaves lose their variegation if the hedge is permanently shaded.

Common beech (Fagus sylvatica) is a superb hedging plant that, although not evergreen, holds on to its warm golden-brown leaves throughout the winter. Its young spring growth is pale green, turning to deep green in summer, so it provides changing interest through the year. An even greater variety can be had by planting a mixture of purple (copper) and green beech plants in one hedge. Beech is happy in most well-drained soils provided they are not too heavy. Where clay predominates it is better to plant the common hornbeam (Carpinus betulus), which also holds its leaves in winter, although they are smaller and duller in colour. Neither species should need clipping more than once a year in summer to keep it in good trim.

There are not a great many flowering shrubs that can be sheared into hedge-shape, but one that can is Berberis darwinii, an evergreen with small holly-like leaves and clusters of orange flowers in April and May that are followed in late summer by purple berries. It can make a dense hedge well over 2 m (6 ft) high, and its sole disadvantage is its prickles. Another good hedging barberry is B. × stenophylla. It forms a dense hedge from which arching branches emerge, bearing golden yellow flowers in April. It should be pruned immediately after flowering. A third barberry, B. gagnepainii lanceifolia, has an erect habit and forms a very narrow but dense hedge about 1.2 m (4 ft) in height. Its narrowness makes it ideal for screening off, say, a vegetable plot in a small garden. The spiny stems carry yellow flowers in spring and, later, blue-black berries. Although evergreen, the narrow leaves take on plum-red tints in the cold months.

The firethorns (Pyracantha), more com-

*A dark hedge makes a good background for emphasising the outline of an ornament or to show off light-coloured flowers. But (inset) there are plenty of brighter hedging plants, like this Japanese honeysuckle (Lonicera nitida 'Baggessons Gold'), to brighten a dull site.*

monly seen as evergreen wall shrubs, can also be trained as hedges. They carry white or cream, hawthorn-like flowers in clusters in June and July and brilliant berries in autumn.

Forsythias can also be used to make a flowering hedge, provided care is taken in the early years to get the base to fill out by means of pruning – or even by tying down some shoots if necessary. It is, of course, a more open shrub and deciduous, so the framework of stems is exposed during the winter. But there are enough examples around to show that it can be kept shapely. The best cultivar for the purpose is probably *Forsythia* × *intermedia* 'Spectabilis', with upright growth and an ability to withstand being clipped two or three times in the summer yet still flower well.

An uncommon but effective flowering hedge can be made from × *Osmarea burkwoodii*, a hardy, compact, slow-growing evergreen shrub that stands up to clipping and shaping. Its oval, dark-green, glossy, leathery leaves are 25–50 mm (1–2 in) long. Small, strongly scented white flowers develop in clusters at the ends and leaf joints of the previous year's shoots in April and May. Once formed the hedge needs no more than an annual clipping in July. This allows time for the new shoots to develop and ripen before the cold weather arrives. Having an appearance rather like a hedge of box, it never looks untidy or overgrown if given this annual trim. *Osmanthus delavayi*, one of its parents, is another useful hedging plant that can be clipped to shape several times in a season. This, too has small, box-like foliage and bears white, scented flowers in April; but it is not fully hardy and is likely to do well only in mild areas of south-west England.

In the 1–1.2 m (3–4 ft) height level, the shrubby cinquefoil (*Potentilla fruticosa*) can be used to create a very effective summer-flowering hedge, blooming as it does from May to the autumn with single white or yellow flowers. It is not evergreen, but makes twiggy growth and can be clipped in winter.

Even shorter, at a mere 450 mm (18 in) or so, the silver-leaved cotton lavender (*Santolina chamaecyparissus*, syn. *S. incana*) can be trained to make a dwarf hedge in town gardens and in milder areas. It makes an effective border to a path and can have its uses in those open-plan front gardens where planting of tall bushes is banned. It bears lemon-yellow flowers in July.

Although much less formal in appearance, roses can make colourful flowering screens. the tall-growing, pink-flowered 'Queen Elizabeth' (a modern shrub rose sometimes grouped with the floribundas) is often used for this purpose, but the older stems can look

rather gaunt; another suitable modern shrub variety is 'Heidelberg', with bright red flowers. Much better are the hybrid musk roses, such as the creamy-salmon 'Penelope' and the coppery-apricot 'Cornelia'. Both are well scented, bloom throughout the summer, and make a hedge 1.2–1.5 m (4–5 ft) high, but you must allow at the very least 1 m (3¼ ft) of space for their width. The site must also be sunny if they are to flower well.

There are many other flowering shrubs that can be used to make informal hedges if you have sufficient room to allow them to develop. Unfortunately, however, space is so often at a premium in modern gardens. As a last resort you can contrive a screen from chestnut paling or chain-link fencing through which the shoots of ivy, honeysuckle, or some other climber are trained. Done with care so that the base is properly filled in, it can be remarkably attractive and certainly does not take up much lateral space, although of course the plants' roots will project out into the soil on either side.

always strongest at the top and so there is a tendency for a hedge to bulge out at the top between clippings. It is much better if the sides are clipped so that they slope inwards slightly towards the top, giving the hedge an 'A' shape when viewed end on. This ensures that the base gets a fair share of light and so remains green and healthy.

All too often established hedges receive no attention other than necessary clipping in summer. Many of them would be better if any rubbish were cleared away from their bases in the autumn and a scattering of bonemeal scratched into the soil around them. On poor and sandy soils a tired hedge often responds well to an annual, early spring dressing of general fertiliser and a 50 mm (2 in) layer of rotted manure, garden compost, or peat laced with bone meal, spread over a strip of soil at least 450 mm (18 in) wide over the root area on both sides. Apart from providing some plant food such a mulch helps conserve soil moisture during the dry summer months.

**Far left** *Golden privet (Ligustrum) gives sunny colour the year round if the site is not too exposed.*

**Near left** *Trim hedges so that sides slope inwards towards the top to prevent the base becoming straggly.*

**Below** *Hybrid-musk rose 'Penelope' makes an attractive, informal hedge that is colourful throughout the summer.*

## Maintenance
It is essential to curb your impatience for height and to trim plants such as privet, laurel, and *Lonicera nitida* regularly during their first full season of growth and thereafter. This is the only way to gain a sound foundation of shoots at the base. If they are allowed to rush straight up without this attention the bottom of the hedge will always be weak and gappy. It is also imperative to destroy weeds to prevent them from smothering the low growth, since this will seriously weaken it and may cause the basal shoots to die out.

The tendency for old hedges to become bare or gappy at the bottom may also be due to letting the top growth overhang the base. Although most people aim for straight, vertical sides when clipping a hedge, growth is

# Broad-Leaved Trees

Trees have a major part to play in any garden by giving height and screening power as well as conferring an air of maturity and permanence. They are also, of course, beautiful in all their varied shapes and sizes. All too often, however, the unwary gardener plants a tree that holds a particular attraction for him or her, without considering its ultimate size. I have lost count of the number of suburban gardens I have seen that are filled to overflowing with a huge, pink-flowering ornamental cherry. There are, in fact, rather few common trees whose growth rate and size at maturity make them suitable for planting in the small garden. Those recommended here are either of naturally modest size or grow slowly enough to remain attractive for many years before becoming too large for the average plot.

There is no way in which you can keep a naturally large, quick-growing tree to a small size when it is planted in a garden. It is possible to have it lopped or pollarded from time to time to reduce the height and spread of the branches, but this cannot be done without ruining the natural appearance of the tree, and there are quite enough hideous examples to be seen in our streets and churchyards already. Far better is to regard larger-growing trees rather in the light of temporary plants. One can then have the enjoyment of a wide variety of specimens for 10, 20, or even more years before they will have to be removed to make way for something new.

One important point to consider when siting any tree that may reach a considerable size is that its roots can extend far through the soil. For this reason it should never be planted close to drains or where the roots could undermine the foundations of buildings. It is not that tree roots physically attack drains and foundations, but they can invade and block a drain if it is defective, and they can absorb moisture from the earth beneath foundations, which may cause the soil to shrink, the foundation to subside, and a wall to crack.

The rate at which trees grow varies enormously and depends not only on the species and cultivar but also on the richness and type of soil and the average annual rainfall. Where I have suggested a size it is an indication of what you might expect after about 15 years of growth. By this time the tree will have passed through its early years, when growth is made quickly, and will have settled down, increasing only slowly as the seasons pass.

## Selection

There are about 200 species of maple (*Acer*), all deciduous, and many of them produce glorious foliage colours in the autumn. Among the finest garden trees are the species native to Japan and China. Arguably the best of all for the smaller garden are the various forms of Japanese maple (*A. palmatum*), which itself is a graceful, slow-growing tree that attains a height of about 4.5 m (15 ft). It needs a naturally moist, well-drained soil and should be protected from cold north and east winds, which tend to frizzle up the new

*If sheltered against cold spring winds that might scorch its young leaves, the Japanese acer (*A. palmatum* 'Atropurpureum') makes an ideal choice even for a very small garden, providing colour with its attractive foliage for many months.*

*Key to plants, pages 110–1: 1 Cotoneaster 'Hybridus Pendulus', 2 Hawthorn (Crataegus oxycantha), 3 Coral-bark maple (Acer palmatum 'Senkaki'), 4 Holly (Ilex), 5 Crab-apple (Malus 'John Downie'), 6 Snowy mespilus (Amelanchier canadensis), 7 Japanese maple (Acer palmatum 'Dissectum Atropupureum'), 8 Willow-leaved pear (Pyrus salicifolia 'Pendula').*

growth in spring. It is difficult to make a choice between the many attractive cultivars. With coppery crimson leaves throughout summer and the vigour to develop quickly into a shapely, fairly upright tree of about 2.5 m (8 ft), *A. palmatum* 'Atropurpureum' is probably the most commonly planted one. But for contrast in a group, *A.p.* 'Dissectum', which grows perhaps half as high, and its even smaller purple-leaved form *A.p.* 'Dissectum Atropurpureum', are more shrubby in habit and rounded in shape. Another group of these elegant maples, *A.p.* 'Heptalobum' in its various forms, develop into spreading trees about 2.1 m (7 ft) high and almost as wide, with horizontal branches. *A.p.* 'Heptalobum Osakazuki', an attractive green in summer, later decks itself in fiery scarlet to outshine all the other Japanese maples, although each colours vividly in autumn.

I cannot leave this charming group of trees without mentioning *A. palmatum* 'Senkaki', the coral-bark maple. When its leaves yellow and fall in autumn they reveal the conspicuous coral-red bark of the younger wood, and this makes an attractive feature until the following season's crop of foliage hides it once again. Beauty of bark is also an attrac-

tion of the paper-bark maple, *A. griseum*. Upright growing, with a dense, rounded head, it reaches a height of about 4.5 m (15 ft) and like many maples puts on a good show of fiery autumn colour before its leaves fall. As the old bark flakes and peels away from the trunk and main branches it reveals the shiny new bark like polished mahogany below.

Although you are often likely to find it listed among shrubs, *A. japonica* 'Aureum' is nonetheless a tree, although it takes years to reach a stature that makes this evident. It is a plant suited to the smallest of plots, where it could grow for half a life-time before it gave

cause for anxiety on account of its height. A compact grower, it fans its soft-yellow foliage out in elegant tiers as its height increases. It has a special advantage over most yellow-leaved trees in that it keeps its colour from spring until the leaves are tinged with red just before they fall; moreover they remain yellow even when growing in shade, which is fortunate since the delicate foliage can be scorched by very strong sunshine.

The snowy mespilus is one of those plants that has had its botanical name changed many times, so that it appears under a variety of guises in catalogues and on nurserymen's labels. The one to which I refer is widely known as *Amelanchier canadensis*, although it may be listed as *A. laevis* or, more properly, *A. lamarckii*. It develops into a slender, compact tree about 4.5 m (15 ft) tall and thrives wherever the soil is neither too hot and dry in summer, nor waterlogged in winter. It has two notable displays a year. The first is in April, when its branches are smothered in white blossom; the second is in September, when its leaves colour richly several weeks before they fall.

One of the most beautiful and striking of all coloured-foliaged trees is the yellow form of the Indian bean tree (*Catalpa bignonoides* 'Aurea'). Its large leaves are broad and shaped rather like the heart symbol on a playing card. Their soft-yellow colour is held throughout the summer and autumn until they fall – unlike so many golden-leaved plants that take on tones of green as the season advances. It is a slow-growing, spreading tree unlikely to exceed a height of 4.5 m (15 ft) in 15 seasons and it can be kept to about 3.7 m (12 ft) by light pruning. Even large specimens will shoot freely from old wood if they have to be cut back hard. This is not a tree to plant in a windy site, however, because of the large leaves, which would be blown into tatters, and the fact that the wood is rather brittle. Because of this it is better suited to a town garden than to an exposed country one. It is not fussy about the soil as long as it is well drained, and it prefers a sunny site. But die-back and frost damage can be a problem in areas with very cold and wet winters and springs.

Better known for its berrying shrubs, the *Cotoneaster* genus also offers garden trees which do well almost anywhere, even on those thin soils overlying chalk and lime-stone. *C.* 'Cornubia' is one with spreading branches and semi-evergreen leaves. It has perhaps the largest red berries of all and, surprisingly, they hang on the tree for months, making a brave show. Size, how-ever, is its disadvantage since its ultimate 6 m (20 ft) width calls for a fair-sized plot. Where

*As well as imparting an air of permanence to a garden, a group of suitably chosen trees provides interesting contrasts of shape and of changing colour as one season gives way to another.*

space is limited, the weeping, 3 m (10 ft) 'Hybridus Pendulus', trained as a small standard, might be chosen. This one is evergreen, its long, trailing branches being clothed with shiny leaves that contrast well with its abundant scarlet fruits.

While most cotoneasters are known for carrying red berries, those of C. 'Exburyensis', another semi-evergreen sometimes available as a standard tree, are creamy yellow. They are carried in clusters and show up even better than red ones, and they often persist until after Christmas.

Hardy and easy-going, doing well even in towns and in seaside locations, the thorns are very adaptable garden trees. Those grown for their blossom are mostly forms of the native white hawthorn or may (*Crataegus oxycantha*). *C.o.* 'Plena' is a double white; *C.o.* 'Rosea Flore Pleno' is a double pink; *C.o.* 'Paul's Scarlet' is a double scarlet. All form well-shaped trees of about 4.5 m (15 ft) in height, usually without any particular attention on the part of the gardener, and flower in May.

Several of the hollies (*Ilex*) are extremely effective for providing year-round colour in a garden. I do not mean the ordinary dark-green kind that is so often stripped of its red berries by the birds long before Christmas, but its relatives with variegated foliage. Their leaves are usually margined with a broad band of yellow or white and look extremely handsome, especially when caught by a ray of winter sunshine. They will attain a height of about 4 m (13 ft) in about 15 years but are quite slow-growing thereafter.

*As the autumn leaves fall from the crab-apple (*Malus*) 'Golden Hornet' the small, brightly coloured fruits gleam in any ray of sunshine.*

Hollies usually carry male and female flowers on different plants, so you will need to have at least one of each if you want berries. But do not be misled by their names: 'Golden King', for instance, is a female cultivar, whereas 'Golden Queen' and 'Silver Queen' are both male.

In June you will find plenty of laburnums opening their yellow pea-shaped flowers, but most of them seem to be rather indifferent seedlings. To have the best display you need to buy a 3.7 m (12 ft) tree of the hybrid cultivar *Laburnum* × *watereri* 'Vossii'. This one bears the longest golden racemes (flower clusters), which sometimes reach a length of 450 mm (18 in), and a tree in full bloom is truly eye-catching. It is essential to plant

laburnums in well-drained soil or they are unlikely to survive for long.

Blossoming in April and May, the flowering crab-apples (Malus) match the ornamental cherries with their display, and follow up with a spectacular crop of fruits. Many cultivars and varieties are grown, and all are perfectly hardy, moderate in size, and quick to settle into a flowering rhythm. Perhaps the best fruiting one is Malus 'John Downie', whose white flowers in May are followed by comparatively large, conical, golden and scarlet crab apples that can be used for making jelly. It forms an open, branching tree some 5.5 m (18 ft) or more tall. M. 'Golden Hornet', also white-flowered, is about as tall but has a more upright shape. Its

fruits are bright yellow in colour and hang on the branches long after the leaves have fallen. M. 'Profusion' is a crab with wine-red flowers and carries a good crop of small crimson fruits in October. It has an added attraction in that the young spring growth is copper coloured at first.

Flowering at about the same time are the Japanese cherries (Prunus). Many of them are lusty growers so you need to select cultivars with care in order to avoid planting trees that will outgrow the space available. All are extremely beautiful in blossom and their shapes vary from spreading to erect. P. 'Okame' reaches some 4.5 m (15 ft) high, but is fairly upright growing. Its bright-pink flowers open as early as March in a mild year.

Laburnum *and lilacs* (Syringa), *which offer good screening power for a town garden, flower at the same season to make a colourful spectacle. Here they are fronted by a hedge of green and golden forms of privet.*

*It is worth taking trouble to site the yellow-leaved false acacia (*Robinia pseudoacacia *'Frisia') against a dark background to accent its glorious foliage.*

Making a compact pyramid-shaped tree of 3 m (10 ft), *P.* × 'Pandora' has soft pink blossom in April. A cultivar suitable for a really small plot is 'Amanogawa' which, having reached a height of 4.5 m (15 ft) after many seasons, will still be no wider than about 600 mm (2 ft). It is a charming sight when its semi-double, pale pink flowers open in May.

Beautiful though these Japanese cherries are, they all suffer one drawback: birds are liable to peck out their buds in winter. In rural areas, especially where bullfinches are common, you may never see many flowers on a tree unless you spray the branches with a bird-repellent. Strange to say one rarely has bird trouble with the winter-flowering autumn cherry (*P. subhirtella* 'Autumnalis'), which bullfinches ignore. This delightful little tree blossoms off and on from November through to April whenever the weather is mild. Although one crop of flowers wreathing its slender stems may be blackened by freezing winds or slashing rain, they are replaced as soon as the weather improves. Obviously its performance can be assisted by giving it a sheltered position, rather than one exposed to the full blast of north and east winds. This form has white semi-double blossom. That of the related cultivar 'Autumnalis Rosea' is a charming pink, but can be somewhat variable; it is as well, therefore, to see what colour pink you are getting before buying a tree. The type species and its cultivars are fairly slow growing, eventually making a tree about 3 m (10 ft) high with a somewhat rounded outline if uncut. But in winter there is always the temptation to visit it, armed with a pair of secateurs, to gather some of the budded sprays that will open indoors if stood in water, just as shoots of winter jasmine do.

One of the most colourful of garden trees you could wish for is *Robinia pseudoacacia* 'Frisia'. Its leaves are bright yellow in colour, without so much as a trace of green, from spring until they fall in the autumn. Against a dark background or planted in association with a deep-purple-leaved shrub, it can make a spectacular sight. Unfussy as to soil type, it should grow quickly to some 5.5 m (18 ft) as long as the site is well drained.

Happy in most places where there is not a lot of lime or chalk, our native mountain ash (*Sorbus aucuparia*) is a good garden tree, although a little too vigorous for many plots. It has given rise to many hybrids and cultivars most of which also have good autumn tints and colourful, berry-like fruits. Although their display is not so brilliant, the trees with yellow or white berries seem to be less attractive to birds in some areas and therefore provide a longer display.

Weeping trees, with their downward sweeping branches, have a special charm of their own. They are often an ideal choice for a small plot because many will increase in height only if the central shoot is tied to a vertical stake or cane each year. Once you stop training them upwards they stay at that height. An obvious exception is the ordinary weeping willow (*Salix babylonica*), which grows ever upwards and outwards as season follows season until it is huge. One of the best of the weeping types is Young's weeping birch (*Betula pendula* 'Youngii'). Another attractive one is the weeping purple beech (*Fagus sylvatica* 'Purpurea Pendula'); much slower-growing than its green counterpart, it is unlikely to outgrow its welcome.

Another excellent weeper for a small plot is the willow-leaved pear (*Pyrus salicifolia* 'Pendula'). If sited against a dark background to accent its outline and show up the silvery foliage, it makes a delightful picture throughout the spring and summer, especially when it is old enough for its branches to sweep the ground. It can get up to about 3.7 m (12 ft) or so in 15 years, but careful pruning of any upward arching shoots will help restrain its height if necessary.

## Maintenance

If properly planted trees are no more difficult to establish in a garden than anything else, but they must be firmly staked. If they are blown about and rocked by the wind, their roots are constantly wrenched and loosened and so never have a chance to establish themselves. The result is at best a sickly tree, at worst a dead one. A really stout stake and an adjustable plastic tree tie may cost almost as much as the tree itself, but are worth it.

The stake must be long enough to reach to just below the 'head' of the tree, so that the whole length of the trunk is supported. Failing that, there is always a danger of the

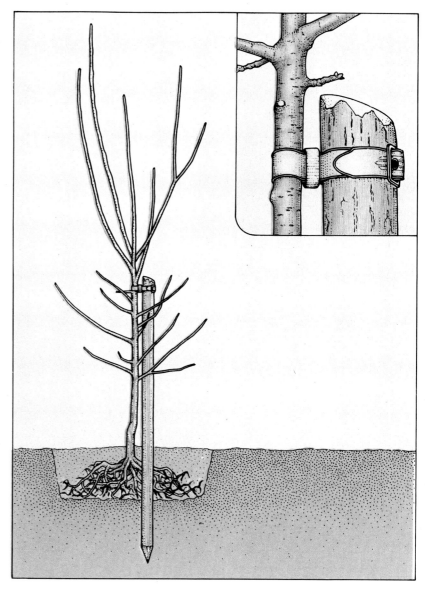

stem snapping just above the topmost tie when the tree breaks into growth and the new shoots and leaves provide the wind with greater leverage. Allow also for at least 600 mm (2 ft) of stake to be buried in the ground to ensure that it remains firm. Drive it into position after excavating the planting hole but before planting the tree, so that you do not damage any roots.

Although you can tie trees to their stakes with soft rope (or even with an old nylon stocking, although this is unsightly), a purpose-made plastic tree tie is best. These are equipped with a buffer that fits between the tree and the stake to prevent chafing. The plastic strap has enough give so as not to strangle the tree as its girth increases, and it can be adjusted by means of a buckle to ensure that the tree is held snugly but never too tightly. Whatever else you may use, *never* tie a tree to a post with the aid of wire, or irretrievable damage may result.

*To give adequate support to a tree a stake must be driven deep into the soil at the base of the planting hole. It is best to attach tree to stake with a purpose-made tie (inset), which provides a buffer between the tree and the stake and can be adjusted to allow for the tree's increasing girth.*

# Conifers

Evergreen conifers are collectively one of the most important groups of trees and shrubs for garden planting. They depend for their impact chiefly on their foliage and overall shape, and because these vary little from one season to the next, the plants help to form the permanent framework of many garden designs. They are especially valuable in winter when they are the main source of massed colour. Evergreen conifers are also extremely useful in their capacity to form a dense screen – not only to hide eyesores, but to create the illusion that a garden is bigger than it really is by disguising the boundary in such a way that the plot appears to continue beyond it. Among their ranks can be found trees varying in shape from neat, straight pillars to spreading bushes and in size from forest giants to completely prostrate forms. Only the slower-growing or smaller kinds are suitable for putting into an average-sized plot, but even they offer immense scope. As with the broad-leaved trees in the previous chapter, all sizes mentioned are what might be expected after 15 years of growth.

## Selection

Perhaps the most commonly seen conifer is Lawson's cypress (*Chamaecyparis lawsoniana*), which is often referred to as 'cupressus'. Left untrained it develops into a tall, cone-shaped tree some 4.5 m (15 ft) or more high, clothed with rather drooping, fanlike foliage. It has given rise to a large number of cultivars that are mostly a little less vigorous of growth and are much more interesting garden trees in colours of rich green, gold, silver, and blue. 'Kilmacurragh' for instance, is bright green, slender, and upright – rather like an Italian cypress in shape – while 'Pottenii' is a pale shade of apple green; 'Green Pillar' lives up to its name and, although it has upward-growing branches, it does not seem to suffer damage as easily as do some trees of this shape when weighed down with snow. Another upright-growing cultivar, 'Columnaris', makes a narrow silvery blue-green pyramid, while 'Ellwoodii', rather less vigorous than the others mentioned, develops into a compact pyramid of feathery grey-blue. One of the bluest of all is 'Pembury Blue', a striking conical tree with sprays of light silvery-blue foliage. Of those cultivars with yellow foliage, which bring the warmth of sunshine to a garden even on dull days, 'Winston Churchill' is richly coloured and carries its golden foliage in winter and summer alike. A little more vigorous, 'Stewartii' is not quite so brilliant, the yellow shading to green at the bases of its branches.

Apart from these trees, *C. lawsoniana* also provides a number of attractive dwarf forms. 'Minima Aurea' is a very slow-growing, rounded bush that holds its yellow foliage fans on edge instead of horizontally as most of the other forms do. For a light touch 'Pygmaea Argentea' ('Backhouse Silver') is similar in shape, but has white tips to its dark-green leaves. But the neatest sphere of all is formed by the blue-green 'Gimbornii'. These three dwarf forms are all slow growing and even 'Gimbornii', which is probably the

*Key to plants, pages 120–1.*
*1 Lawson's cypress*
*(Chamaecyparis*
*lawsoniana)*
*'Kilmacurragh', 2 Lawson's*
*cypress 'Columnaris',*
*3 Lawson's cypress 'Green*
*Pillar', 4 Lawson's cypress*
*'Pottenii', 5 Lawson's cypress*
*'Gimbornii', 6 Lawson's*
*cypress 'Columnaris Glauca',*
*7 Colorado spruce (Picea*
*pungens 'Koster'),*
*8 Westfelton yew (Taxus*
*baccata 'Dovastonii'),*
*9 Sawara cypress*
*(Chamaecyparis pisifera*
*'Filifera Aurea'), 10 Chinese*
*juniper (Juniperus*
*chinensis 'Pfizeriana*
*Aurea').*

most vigorous, is unlikely to grow to much more than 600 mm (2 ft) across in ten seasons. Where a small conical tree is wanted, 'Ellwood's Pillar' might fit the bill; this is a scaled-down version of *C.l.* 'Ellwoodii' and is unlikely to exceed 1 m (3¼ ft) in height after a decade.

The various forms of the Sawara cypress (*C. pisifera*) are very different from other conifers in that they have thread-like branchlets. This feature is most striking in the yellow forms, such as 'Filifera Aurea' and 'Gold Spangle', which eventually make mounds of golden filigree. Both of these are slow growing, but whereas 'Filifera Aurea' is unlikely to make a bush greater than 1 m (3¼ ft) in height, 'Gold Spangle' can eventually become much larger.

Junipers also provide an extremely wide selection of shapes and colours to tempt a gardener. A perfect gem for a rock garden is to be found in *Juniperus communis* 'Compressa', which slowly grows into a tiny, compact, green column 450 mm (18 in) high. Of the same shape, but on a much larger scale, is the Irish juniper (*J. c.* 'Hibernica'), which climbs to about 2.7 m (9 ft) in height after many years, keeping its slim outline quite naturally. *J. c.* 'Depressa Aurea', on the other hand, is a dwarf, spreading plant. Its feathery-looking, yellow spring growth deepens to gold in the summer and turns to bronze as the days become colder.

*J. horizontalis* is a creeping juniper and provides a number of colourful cultivars. One of the most brilliant is 'Blue Moon', its feathery-looking foliage being bright silver-blue in summer, changing to a greyish tone in winter. Quite vigorous, it can spread over 1.5 m (5 ft) across in 10 years or so. A little more vigorous is 'Emerald Spreader', a completely prostrate form with bright emerald-green foliage.

Under *J. × media* (syn. *J. chinensis*) are listed a number of natural hybrids. 'Blaauw', at 1.2 m (4 ft), is unusual in that it has upright feathery branches that splay out a little from the centre, eventually to form a distinct vase shape. Its foliage colour, a good blue-green, is retained throughout the year. 'Pfitzeriana Aurea' is a low bush with all-but-horizontal branches spreading one over another. The new growth is yellow in summer but tones down to greenish yellow for the winter. It has given rise to a natural mutation called 'Old Gold', with only about one third of the growth rate of its parent, but of a deeper golden colour which does not green up in the winter months.

Silvery blue is the colour of the Nepal juniper (*J. squamata* 'Blue Star'), which eventually forms a compact hummock of

branches that are given a rather spiky appearance by the bright leaves. It is hardly likely to outgrow its allotted space since it may take 10 years to reach a spread of 300 mm (1 ft) or a height of 250 mm (10 in). But although it is diminutive in size, its colour ensures it never goes unnoticed.

Mention of spruce (*Picea*) may make you think of Christmas trees, but the genus has many garden-worthy forms in its ranks. The Christmas tree, or Norway spruce (*P. abies*, syn. *P. excelsa*), has provided a number of cultivars, all slow-growing, that make neat, rounded little bushes, suitable for even the tiniest of plots. Good examples are *P. abies* 'Little Gem', a bright-green, mop-like bush only 300 mm (1 ft) high and a little wider, and the dark-green *P. a.* 'Nidiformis', or bird's-nest spruce (so called because of the central depression that forms in the top of the young bush), which grows to perhaps half as big again.

Eye-catching is certainly the right term for the Caucasian spruce (*P. orientalis* 'Aurea'). This one has a similar appearance to the

*One of the many forms of Lawson's cypress (Chamaecyparis lawsoniana), 'Pembury Blue' is a moderate grower that eventually assumes a cone-shaped outline.*

*A combined planting of various conifers and ground-covering heathers, as shown here, guarantees year-round colour and interest for a minimum of maintenance.*

ordinary Christmas tree spruce, but puts on a startling display in spring when the very pale yellow new growth shows up against the dark green of the rest of the foliage. These new shoots gradually turn gold, then green, although the tree never completely loses a hint of sunniness. This is not a tree for a very small plot unless you are prepared to replace it after about 10 years, when its height will be 3 m (10 ft) or so.

Making a strong claim as possessing the most brilliant blue of all conifers are the forms of the Colorado spruce (*P. pungens*). The cultivar 'Globosa' makes a dense, flat-topped little bush about 600 m (2 ft) high and wide with silver-blue needles. 'Koster' slowly develops into a slender, conical tree some 3 m (10 ft) high that holds its intense silver-blue colour throughout the year.

No look at garden conifers would be complete without a quick glance at the yews (*Taxus*). Those huge, centuries-old trees sometimes seen in graveyards are the common yew (*Taxus baccata*), but you probably would not recognise it as the originator of the cultivar called 'Repens Aurea', a dwarf, prostrate, golden-leaved form; nor of 'Semperaurea', which makes a dense bush clothed with bright gold and cream foliage in winter and summer. Those imposing Irish yews that form a neat column of erect branches are *T. baccata* 'Fastigiata'. The form 'Fastigiata Aureomarginata' offers a lighter touch, the young growth appearing first yellow, but toning down as the gold recedes to the leaf margins only. For a tiny, very narrow, golden pillar that will shine out in the dark winter days, the extremely slow-growing, dwarf *T. b.* 'Standishii' would fit the bill in any size of garden. It takes about 10 seasons to reach the dizzy height of 1 m (3¼ ft).

Bushes that also maintain more than a hint of sun in their year-round colouring are to be found among the cultivars of the arbor-vitae (*Thuja occidentalis*). 'Rheingold' makes a feathery looking, rather pointed bush. In summer it is a pale yellow, but this changes to a rich old gold in the winter months to enliven the dullest of days. Slow growing, it may take 20 years to reach 2 m (6½ ft). Another is 'Aurea Nana', which holds its foliage sprays on edge, forming a fat, oval, yellow-green bush; even slower to develop, it may take a decade to top 600 mm (2 ft). Somewhat freer growing, 'Conspicua' may reach 4 m (13 ft) in about 12 years. Conical in shape, it makes a dense bush which holds its golden colour through the winter.

Although all the conifers so far mentioned have been upright or spreading, bushy or prostrate, they can also offer one or two very attractive trees of weeping appearance. The Nootka cypress (*Chamaecyparis nootkatensis* 'Pendula') is particularly spectacular as a young tree, when its outstretched branches radiating from an upright trunk are festooned with hanging branchlets and foliage.

The coffin juniper (*Juniperus recurva coxii*) is a true weeper, its branches sweeping gracefully downwards from the central stem. It is one of those conifers that can eventually grow very tall, but seems to be so slow growing that you could enjoy it for perhaps half a lifetime in quite a small garden before it had to be taken out.

One of the most spectacular conifers, although regrettably not one of the easiest to establish and certainly not one for a windy site, is Brewer's spruce (*Picea breweriana*). Its basic outline is conical, with downward-curving branches that are fringed with long hanging branchlets of blue-green foliage. It makes a spectacular specimen tree and although its ultimate size is large, it is slow to develop and may well reach no higher than 2 m (6 ft) in its first 10 years of life.

A much easier to grow conifer of weeping appearance that thrives in sun or shade is the Westfelton yew (*Taxus baccata* 'Dovastonii'). This makes an attractive small tree with horizontal branches that are festooned with weeping branchlets; the foliage is very deep green. 'Dovastonii Aurea' is of similar appearance but with yellow-edged leaves.

## Maintenance

Most conifers grow well in most types of soil, provided that they are neither shallow nor dry. Yews thrive where there is chalk and on quite thin soils, too, while the junipers can do well in surprisingly dry, sandy and chalky soils. The thujas, on the other hand, show a preference for a much heavier rooting medium and a high rainfall area.

The great majority of conifers should be sited so that they enjoy plenty of sun. If kept in the shade of other trees they tend to elongate too quickly and the yellow forms, especially, lose colour and become more green as the shade deepens.

Most conifers require little in the way of pruning or training, taking on the various shapes quite naturally. The prostrate forms are often better if the leading shoots are lightly pruned to encourage them to thicken out rather than to wander too far afield at first. If an all-green shoot appears on a coloured-leaved form it must be cut out entirely. Occasionally a conifer with a distinct trunk may develop two or more shoots at the apex instead of just a single leading shoot. If left to grow these would ruin the tree's shape, and all but the best shoots should be shortened or removed. It is sometimes

necessary, with a young tree, to tie the leading shoot to a cane to keep it straight and encourage upward development for two or three seasons.

In common with other evergreens, all these plants are either pot-grown or specially treated in the nursery to encourage the formation of a dense, fibrous root system so that they can be transplanted with a large amount of their roots encased in a ball of soil. Every effort must be made to keep this ball of roots and soil intact at planting time. To help keep it moist, wet peat should be packed around it when planting and, after the soil is trodden firm around it, the site should be liberally watered, and then covered with a 50 mm (2 in) mulch of peat. Check occasionally to see that the root ball does not dry out while new roots are pushing out into the surrounding soil, and water around the base of the plant if necessary to rewet it. Such care is needed because, while all plants inevitably lose some of their roots system when they are transplanted, conifers, like all evergreens, continue to lose moisture from their leaves – and

this has to be made good by the remaining roots if the plants are not to suffer a setback.

One of the biggest enemies of newly transplanted conifers is a dry wind, which desiccates the plants before they can make sufficient new roots to supply their full water needs. It pays, therefore, to screen them for a few weeks from drying winds with sacking or sheet polythene arranged around stakes or canes. You can also speed their establishment, and increase the growth rate in the first year, if you wet their foliage by syringing or spraying them overhead with water on the evenings of dry days.

Another enemy of conifers, particularly those with upright-growing branches, is snow, which can weigh them down and spoil their shape, or even snap off whole branches. After a heavy fall it is worth knocking off as much snow as you can from your conifers with a broom. And to avoid the upright ones being spoiled, it pays to ring them round with stout wire in the autumn to prevent the possibility of their branches splaying out under the additional weight.

*Landscaping in miniature is possible with dwarf conifers. A variety of shapes, forms, and colours is available.*

# INDEX

## ACKNOWLEDGEMENTS

The publishers wish to thank the following for their kind permission to reproduce the photographs in this book: **Bernard Alfieri** 13; **Pat Brindley** 28, 53, 57 below, 127; **Bruce Coleman Ltd (E. Crichton)** 1, 90–1, 114–5, 116–7, **(H.R. Heyer)** 49; **Iris Hardwick Library** 16–17, 40, 51; **Jerry Harpur** 2–3, 4–5, 20–1, 77, 78–9, 106–7; **G.E. Hyde** 105 inset; **Palma Studio** 22–3, 71, 81, 124–5; **Harry Smith Photographic Collection** 41, 85 inset, 89 inset, 95 above, 98–9, 100, 105, 109, 118; **Michael Warren** 27, 29, 30–1, 35, 36, 37, 38, 42–3, 47, 50, 52, 57 above, 58, 59, 60, 61, 67, 72, 73, 74 and inset, 75, 80, 85, 86, 87, 89, 95 below, 96, 97, 101 above and below, 107 inset, 113, 116 left, 123; **George Wright** 11, 18, 62–3, 65, 88, 108.
Illustrators **Nicholas Hall** 12, 39, 66, 109, 119; **Technical Arts Services** 8, 16, 26, 34, 46, 56, 70, 84, 94, 104, 112, 122; **Elsie Wrigley** 24–5, 32–3, 44–5, 54–5, 69–9; **Paul Wrigley** 6–7, 14–15, 21–2, 82–3, 102–3, 110–1, 120–1.
Garden plans by **Elsie Wrigley**.